naturally NORDIC

naturally NORDIC

THE RUSTIC CHARM OF COUNTRY LIVING

Niki Brantmark

photography by James Gardiner

CICO BOOKS

For Olivia, Alice, and Albin

This edition published in 2026 by CICO Books
An imprint of Ryland Peters & Small Ltd
20–21 Jockey's Fields, London WC1R 4BW
www.rylandpeters.com
Email: euregulations@rylandpeters.com

10 9 8 7 6 5 4 3 2 1

First published in 2016 under the title *Modern Pastoral*

A CIP record for this book is available from the British Library. US Library of Congress CIP data has been applied for.

ISBN: 978 1 78879 773 3

Printed in China

Editor: Gillian Haslam
Designer: Louise Leffler
Photographer: James Gardiner
See page 176 for additional photography credits.

Senior editor: Carmel Edmonds
Art director: Sally Powell
Head of production: Patricia Harrington
Publishing manager: Penny Craig
Publisher: Cindy Richards

The authorised representative in the EEA is
Authorised Rep Compliance Ltd.,
Ground Floor, 71 Lower Baggot Street,
Dublin, D01 P593, Ireland
www.arccompliance.com

FSC www.fsc.org MIX Paper | Supporting responsible forestry FSC® C106563

contents

INTRODUCTION

"Delight in the beauty that surrounds you." ANON.

When I was a child, my family saw weekends and school vacations as an opportunity to exchange the hustle and bustle of London for the tranquility of the English countryside. I have particularly vivid memories of Easters in the Lake District, in the north of England. I remember the rain-soaked landscape, the rugged mountains, and the black-faced sheep who gazed at us curiously as we wandered by in our waterproofs and boots. On sunny days, my older sister and I would build dams in the stream at the foot of the garden or collect wild flowers (my sister) and snails (me). Our home for the week's vacation was a small stone cottage with an old-fashioned electricity meter that devoured coins.

Although I didn't realize it at the time, I can now see that an essential ingredient of these weeks away was going "back-to-basics." We were together as a family, surrounded by nature, with its free and simple pleasures.

Today, the desire to lead a simpler life is growing and rural homes are becoming increasingly popular. However, in this book there is something very different about these residences from the archetypal country-style home. Whether in the form of a summer cottage on the north coast of Zealand, Denmark, a country home in Skåne, southern Sweden, or a barn conversion in the Catskill Mountains, the "modern pastoral" home is designed to reconnect with nature and the immediate surroundings.

The ten pastoral homes I explored for this book may not be as basic as that stone cottage in the Lake District—many display modern comforts such as espresso machines, televisions, and a well-stocked bar. However, the furnishings are artfully simple, purposeful, and pared-back. The furniture may be found in local flea markets or made of reclaimed or repurposed bits and pieces from a nearby barn. We encountered magnificent tables assembled from old floorboards or slabs of oak, designed to accommodate large gatherings over a feast of foraged or homegrown food.

The home is often built or restored using materials that harmonize with the landscape and adhere to the heritage of the home. Pine in a modern log cabin in Denmark, bluestone in a cottage in the Hudson Valley, and limestone in a farmhouse in southern Sweden are typical examples. Large windows and sliding doors are designed to offer unobstructed views and reveal the magnificence of the surrounding countryside.

Plants, flowers, sheepskin rugs, cowhides, skulls, feathers, and pebbles all play a part in connecting the home with its environment, and creating a sense of continuity between the outside and inside. The decorative details can be as simple as a basket of freshly laid eggs on the sideboard, a dried honeycomb found on the ground in winter, or a piece of driftwood washed up from a nearby river.

All these homes have distinct themes that can be associated with nature. Homes inspired by the "Forest" are dark, with pops of red or orange provided by a pitcher or blanket standing out against a backdrop of exposed timber walls. "Graphical" interiors conjure up a winter's day and the black silhouette of a tree against a backdrop of snow. By contrast, the "Homestead" style is made up of rich autumnal browns like those found in horse chestnuts, offset by calm neutrals, beiges, and whites. Finally, the soothing "Waterside" homes are based on blues and grays, and warmed with natural wood and rattan.

While compiling this book, I've been exposed to lots of ingenious ideas, many of them simple and highly original. These have inspired me to display the pebbles, shells, sticks, and feathers my daughters collect in a whole new way. My sideboards are overflowing with whatever plants and flowers are available in the garden at the time. When I catch sight of these items, I am briefly transported back to a world where nature is the only distraction, back to my own childhood and those carefree days by the stream.

Whether you are in the process of renovating a rural home or simply looking for fresh ways to bring a small part of nature into your city residence, I hope this book inspires you to "delight in the beauty that surrounds you." You, too, can create a haven where it is possible to switch off and luxuriate—albeit temporarily—in life's simpler pleasures.

CHAPTER ONE

forest

Inspired by the deep forest where warm, dark brown wood merges with a myriad of greens, pierced by the brilliant flash of color from a beautiful bird or a majestic stag. Exposed timber walls are lit by shafts of natural light, bringing life to the rich colors and textures, providing a backdrop for traditional patterns, woven rugs, and a cozy wood-burning stove. A bright red vase, dried yarrow from the field, or golden corn from last year's harvest add a pop of color.

MILKWEED BARN

Bill Hovard's sharp eye for design, his passion for primitive American artifacts, and his love for the countryside have successfully merged in this rural upstate New York barn conversion. Over the space of eight years, a simple early 19th-century farm building has been artfully transformed into a beautiful, dynamic 21st-century home. Milkweed Barn is a triumphant blend of past and present, and the perfect retreat from which to enjoy the fresh green pastures and dense forests of the Catskill Mountains in Delaware County.

When Bill first acquired this stunning barn just outside the small hamlet of South Kortright, it was in need of total renovation, but the breathtaking countryside with its pristine green pastures and thickly forested undulating hills proffered the peace and tranquility he was looking for. The awe-inspiring Dutch-style barn was originally part of a larger farm, and served as a hayloft and stalls for horses and cows. The original structure, made from old-growth virgin forests and hand-hewn pegged posts and beams, nestles into the land on a foundation of locally quarried bluestone. The striking exterior siding is made from natural northern hemlock, and each of the four facades has gracefully aged, changing color according to its orientation. Toward the south, a milk house—originally used for cooling milk on the farm—is still present today.

Throughout the year magnificent flocks of birds, ranging from wrens, bluebirds, and robins to larger birds of prey, such as bald eagles, glide and swoop over the landscape. The sound

Opposite: The weathered wood siding on the east-facing facade of Milkweed Barn has been tarnished black over the years, making a striking contrast with the lush green surrounds.

Right: The charming, unstructured nature of a pretty stone woodland path reflects the relaxed nature of the home.

of a woodpecker can be heard chiseling away somewhere high up in the eaves of the barn, while outside beavers, coyotes, raccoons, skunks, bears, and deer make their presence known as they wander past the house. Milkweed was found to be growing freely in the seven acres of land, attracting clouds of Monarch butterflies on their migration south, prompting the moniker Milkweed Barn.

Bill set about painstakingly transforming the barn into a modern home while being careful to preserve the integrity of the building. Work was carried out using locally sourced materials consistent with the barn's heritage. Reclaimed barn siding and

Above left: An old knife-sharpening tool rests against the front of the house, serving as an important reminder of the barn's heritage as a working farm.
Above: A collection of glass milk bottles, dating back to the 1930s and 1950s, sits on a windowsill in the former milk house, a touching tribute to the past.
Opposite: Bill is a keen cook and grows fresh produce such as rhubarb, kale, and tomatoes in raised beds to use as ingredients in the kitchen.

oak posts have been sourced to replace or reinforce parts of the original structure. Materials such as quarried bluestone have been used to create kitchen work surfaces and a tabletop in the sitting room, with cherry wood used in the kitchen cabinetry and for the flooring throughout the top floor.

Bill is a keen collector and is particularly fond of mid-century furniture and 18th-century primitive American artifacts. However, as a neatnik, he ensures that the items are carefully edited to ensure a clutter free living space. The home is simply furnished with handmade furniture from the region complemented by a selection of handpicked, dual-purpose mid-century pieces, found at various auctions and yard sales. Throughout the home, an eclectic mix of unassuming objects, including farming tools and artwork, pay homage to the barn's original function. The diverse mix of furniture, knickknacks, and décor has been kept to a primarily neutral color scheme. The result is a stunning, comfortable, unified living space, which strikes the perfect balance between the past and the present.

Opposite: The large dining table was salvaged from Bill's office in New York, where it had served as a conference table. Maintenance has deliberately slipped to allow it to grow old gracefully, blending into its new life as a farmhouse table. Today it is used multi-functionally for cooking, baking, and entertaining, and represents the heart of the home. The benches made by a local carpenter complement the simple nature of the space and provide a versatile seating arrangement.

Above left: Chopping boards from Bill's company, Hudson Made, hang in a row on the back wall of the kitchen. The pieces are made from locally sourced black walnut and combine traditional craftsmanship with modern design. Rhubarb from the vegetable patch is kept fresh in a vase of water.

Above center: A meat hook found in an antique store hangs from a nail as decoration.

Above right: Hudson Made linen and twill aprons are kept to hand on the wall of the kitchen. Above, a horseshoe found on the property rests on a beam, a reminder of the horses once stabled there.

3

Formerly the farmyard stalls, the ground floor has been transformed into a large open-plan living space comprising a sitting room, dining area, and kitchen. Exposed timber walls, eye-catching posts and beams, and a 40-foot (13-meter) high ceiling create a dramatic backdrop for the spacious sitting room. The comfortable seating area is decorated with natural materials to blend with the environment, with a leather sofa and mid-century chair re-upholstered in unbleached cotton canvas surrounding a coffee table. In the background, a 19th-century cabinet, sourced in the Catskill Mountains, is used to store and display Bill's pottery collection.

Previous page, left: A small selection from Bill's extensive traditional American crockery collection is kept on display atop the large masonry oven.

Previous page, right: A vast masonry oven radiates heat long after the fire has died, helping to keep the barn warm in winter. The upper chamber can be used to cook stews and bake fresh bread. A pair of locally sourced antlers decorates the wall in between the entrance hall and kitchen.

Above: Pots and pans, ready for use, hang on nails from a horizontal beam in the kitchen.

Opposite: A traditional cast-iron wood-burning stove helps heat the ground floor in winter. Kindling is kept to hand in a vintage container, while larger logs are stacked behind. A slab of local bluestone protects the floor from heat.

HearthStone

A cleverly placed mid-century dresser divides the sitting room from the kitchen. The top level of the dresser slides open to reveal a black lacquer surface. Formerly used as a bar for entertaining, it is now used to display an ever-changing array of decorative items, such as Japanese teapots and Scandinavian ceramics.

In the winter, when temperatures can reach as low as a biting -22°F (-30°C), a wood-burning stove in the back corner of the room is fired into action. The small stove complements a much larger masonry oven situated in the main entrance, and this striking Finnish-designed oven acts like a furnace, providing the primary source of heat for the huge barn. This is supplemented by a Propane-fueled heating system, feeding black cast-iron radiators dotted around the house. Next to the oven is a 1940s glass cabinet, used for displaying fragile items such as birds' nests, feathers, and bones found in the grounds of the property. A large off-white shag pile rug anchors the space, creating a warm and inviting atmosphere.

The kitchen is in a more modern section of the living space, and Bill has been careful not to mask this, making a feature of the contemporary feel. The walls are painted fresh white and subway tiles adorn the walls behind the sink. The light, airy, contemporary look and feel juxtapose with the original, darker rustic area of the sitting room, adding much-needed light and creating a distinct zone.

Bill has forged close ties with the local community and loves to entertain using produce from his garden or sourced from nearby farms. Consistent with the rest of the house, the kitchen has been functionally equipped with items that blend into the overall style of the barn. A deep farmers' sink offers enough

Opposite: Bill admires mid-century furniture for its amalgamation of form and function. This beautiful mid-century dresser can be used as a bar or for storage. On top, a vibrant bouquet of yellow foxtail lilies sits alongside pottery by mid-century Swedish artist Berndt Friberg. **Above:** A collection of Japanese teapots and a set of wooden spoons from Tanzania have been neatly arranged on a tray to create an interesting display.

space to wash masses of fresh produce, or to cope with the demands of dish washing after a large dinner party. Huge chopping boards hang behind the sink and are used to prepare food and then double up as serving platters. Decorated with a vase filled with dried yarrow from Bill's garden, the large dining table can seat up to 14 guests. Overhead, a large round pendant light breaks up the clean, straight lines of the kitchen, emphasizing the contemporary feel.

Dramatic hand-hewn stairs run the length of the open-plan living space, cutting it in two and leading up to the sleeping quarters. Originally the hayloft, the master bedroom has been transformed into a large lofty room, with a double bed looking up into the timber eaves of the barn. The look is clean and uncluttered, the neutral colors making a beautiful contrast with the darkness of the wood. Simple,

Opposite left: Printing blocks from an old letterpress rest on a wooden beam in the sitting room, as a nod to Bill's long career as a creative director.

Opposite right: A knife holster and cattle bridle purchased at auction pay homage to the original function of the sitting room, as a stall for horses and cows.

Above left: A charming potato shopping bag found at auction has been given a new lease on life as a playful "print" on the wall of the barn. A traditional circular sieve adds to the farming theme.

Above: An antique German fish poster and small-scale antlers adorn the wall, reflecting the abundance of wildlife in the surrounding Catskill Mountains.

handcrafted blocks of oak have been used as night tables and a large shagpile rug brings a touch of luxury to the room. A collection of glass medicine bottles decorates the top of a vintage stereo system, which still functions as a record player and radio today.

At first, the barn was used as a weekend retreat, helping Bill to seek the balance he craved between frenetic life in New York, where he worked as a designer and creative director, and the tranquility of nature. But over time he found himself becoming more and more immersed in the farming and creative communities in Hudson Valley and the Catskill Mountains, so he founded Hudson Made, a company manufacturing and selling regional and locally made artisanal soaps, aprons, and kitchen boards.

With nothing tying him to the city, in 2013 Bill took the decision to move permanently to Milkweed Barn. Depending on the time of year, he can be found tending to his Hudson Made botanical crops, including calendula, yarrow, and chamomile, which are used in some of the products, or running his business from the basement of the barn. In the evenings he climbs the stairs to his living quarters where he enjoys relaxing, looking out over the magnificent Catskill Mountain scenery, entertaining guests, or simply taking in the peace of his surroundings.

Previous pages: The sitting room is flooded with natural light from two aspects. A large contemporary rug anchors the space, to form a designated seating area. A locally sourced cabinet, thought to be salvaged from a clerk's office, blends into the back wall. Today the cubbyholes and pockets are home to fragile items, including 19th-century red ware and mid-century Scandinavian pottery.
Above left: The subtle colors, shapes, and markings on rare hand-blown medicinal bottles make a beautiful display on an otherwise disused surface.
Opposite: The neutral color scheme and minimalist nature of the bedroom create a calm oasis in which to wake up each morning. The lofty height of the room is offset by the timber structure and wood floor, which work together to form a cozy, cabin-like feel.

NORTH PARK

MODERN LOG HOUSE

At first sight, this Danish family holiday home on the shores of the Kattegat Sea, on the northern coast of Zealand, looks like a magnificent piece of modern architecture. Dig deeper though, and the timber, glass, and steel construction conceals a traditional way of living, where the great outdoors and family togetherness lie at the core. The result is a truly unique modern log house where rustic charm and a minimalist lifestyle combine with clean lines for a contemporary spin on the time-honored Nordic log cabin.

Owner and architect Jesper Brask acquired the acre of woodland in 2007, and he and his family of five moved into a small 32-feet (10-meter) square wooden "wagon" at the foot of the garden (seen on page 47) to oversee the build. Over the next two years, the family grew to love the confined living space. Surrounded by few belongings and simple furnishings, this lifestyle provided them with a wonderful feeling of contentment. They appreciated the amount of time spent outdoors, the feeling of peace, and the rich woodland. The natural surroundings became an integral part of their everyday life and, in a sense, their home. They were keen to preserve this magical way of life and, as a result, these factors have played a significant role in the overall design of the main house today.

Opposite: The large wood deck is considered part of the living space. Wall-to-wall sliding glass doors create a seamless flow between inside and out and flood the room with natural light.
Above: A row of windows immediately under the eaves creates the illusion of a floating roof. Huge windowpanes at the side of the house reflect the Austrian pines, blending the home in with its surroundings.

Jesper turned to traditional Nordic log-cabin design for inspiration. These dwellings were built from natural, untreated wood, which was, and still is, a plentiful resource in northern Europe today. Inside, the living space was centered around a hearth, which provided warmth, a place to cook, and somewhere for the family to gather and share stories.

The Brask family's modern log house has been built in much the same way. A vast chimney takes center stage in a communal living area. The chimney contains three fireplaces: a wood-burning stove (the main source of heat for the house in colder months), an outdoor fireplace for evenings alfresco, and a third "oven" in the kitchen for cooking. The chimneybreast also cleverly conceals modern-day essentials, such as the fridge and dishwasher, while a concrete bar table doubles up as a work surface and a place for a sink and stove. Two stools

Opposite: A large wooden daybed on wheels can easily be transported outdoors and moved around the garden, depending on the light and time of day. A rustic tree stump from the land is used as a side table.

Above left: Checked blankets found at various flea markets are neatly stored in a large wicker basket, ready to be used at whim.

Above: Kayaking along the coast is one of the many activities the family enjoys at the house. A pile of recently chopped firewood is kept dry under the eaves.

Overleaf, left: Steel transcends the house, emphasizing the seamlessness between indoors and out. The sturdy material is able to support an elegantly slim roof, which extends over the terrace on either side of the house.

Overleaf, right: A round white concrete bar table engrained with small Norwegian stones is set into the chimneybreast. This versatile surface is used for preparing and cooking food.

provide a place to sit and socialize. The result is a fascinating and ingenious modern take on the traditional hearth.

The house itself is largely made from Austrian pine trees felled from the land on which it stands. The logs were dried for two years, stripped, and squared off (in the past the logs would have been employed in their original round form), before being used in the final construction. The smooth, natural texture of the pine can be seen on the exterior and interior of the house, adding a wonderful rustic touch. A contemporary exposed steel structure supports the timber wall and also facilitates the use of large expanses of glass, which draw nature indoors. The tremendous two-pitched floor-to-ceiling windows flood the house with light and, combined with the shade from the trees, the northwest orientation ensures the living area always remains cool. From the outside, the windows act like vast mirrors, reflecting the lush green trees and creating a camouflage affect, helping the home to blend in with its surroundings.

Wall-to-wall sliding glass doors open right back to create a smooth transition between inside and out. The eaves of the streamlined, remarkably thin roof extend right out over the wood decking on either side of the house, creating covered terraces that double up as extra living space in warmer months.

Opposite: With its green mattress and pillows, the daybed blends into the vibrant green foliage of the garden behind, creating the illusion that it is outdoors. A wood-burning stove keeps the sitting area warm in winter.
Above left: None of the wood chopped down to create space for the house was wasted. Here a tree stump has been used as a convenient place for a tin pitcher and mugs, found at a flea market.
Overleaf: Family and friends gather around a long dining table made by a local carpenter. The practical table can be extended to more than 13 feet (4 meters) in length to accommodate larger parties and has built-in wheels so that it can be transported outside for alfresco dining. Overhead shelving is used to display kitchen items collected over the years and reflects the relaxed, open feel of the home.

The seamless blending of interior and exterior helps to maintain the wonderful outdoor life to which the family has become so accustomed.

Inspired by the "wagon" the family originally lived in, the home has been simply furnished. Much of the furniture and storage has been built in to the construction, using wood from the land. Windows are undressed to allow the spectacular uninterrupted views of the woodland to dominate the living space. The timber walls have deliberately been kept picture free to allow the beauty of the uneven texture and variety in color to shine through and become decoration in their own right. The only personal touch can be seen on the bathroom door, which has been completely covered by a striking blown-up black-and-white photograph of the three sons wading out to sea, taken by Jesper at the nearby beach.

Opposite: Sliding doors are a great way to save space. The bathroom door has been covered with an enlarged photo of the three sons in the sea—an immensely personal and clever way to bring the seascape indoors.

Above left: Hats and bags are hung on hooks from the exposed steel construction in the bedroom.

Above: The beautiful rich texture and color variation in the timber construction plays a central role in the décor.

The exposed steel structure can be seen throughout the living space, bringing a cool, modern, industrial vibe to the interior. The beams double up as support for open-plan shelving. Hooks have been inserted into the holes of the steel beams and posts to create a natural place to hang hats, coats, and bags, and even keys and other small items.

The color scheme has been kept equally understated. A simple handmade built-in daybed/sofa spans the width of the northwest facing window. It's been minimally dressed with a green mattress and pillows to blend with the foliage outside. The modern piece has been cleverly positioned under the dual-

Opposite: Bedrooms are pared back and fuss-free in keeping with the nature of the home. Fresh white bed linen and a simple rag rug allow the timber wall to become the main feature of the room.
Above left: A vase of dahlias livens up the night table and picks up the green of the woodland outside the window.
Above: The magnificent architecture is one of the outstanding features of the living space. Windows span the full height of the wall and part of the ceiling to create an almost magical feeling of living under the boughs of the trees, bathing the environment in plenty of natural light.

pitched window to create the illusion of lying outside, gazing up into the boughs of the Austrian pines. A simple tree stump from the grounds is used as a table for books and a cup of coffee. A brightly checked blanket is kept at hand for cooler days and provides the only real pop of color. Jesper likens this splash of color in blankets and other accessories to a bouquet of flowers—items that can be changed and moved around, or even discarded, according to the mood and season.

The only other flash of color within the room stems from ceramics, glassware, and other household items randomly displayed upon open shelving running the length of the back wall. This arrangement reinforces the relaxed atmosphere of the dining area. A long wooden pine table, made by a local carpenter from the well-stocked wood shed, provides a place for friends and family to gather at mealtimes. A set of 1960s red and yellow vintage dining chairs found at auction are positioned at either end and along one side of the table. The relaxed, understated nature of the chairs fits with the easy feel of the room. On the other side, a long wooden bench, built into the wall, provides both seating and storage space. Two round modern pendant lamps hang over the table, matching the rounded concrete bar table on the opposite side of the room. The gray shade works in harmony with the steel structure exposed in the wall behind.

At night the family retires to private bedrooms leading off the communal area. In one, the natural, rustic pine wall creates a cozy feel, with a simple tree trunk repurposed into a night table, bringing in an element of the outdoors. A green pillow and flowers introduce a touch of color, while a single rug adds softness to the space. Clothes are hidden from view in low, built-in storage cabinets for a fuss-free look, cleverly doubling up as a side table for a reading lamp and magazines.

A simple wooden ladder leads up from the open-plan living space to a mezzanine level and the third bedroom. The bed is surrounded by floor-to-ceiling windows, creating the magical feeling of sleeping under a canopy of stars. In the daytime it serves as a comfy place to read, play card games, or simply look out over the open-plan living space below. The garden, which also contains a guesthouse, is as much a part of

A glass-walled, loft-style room has been built above the open-plan dining area, providing a magical place to relax or sleep on the inviting platform bed high among the trees.

Opposite: A mattress on the floor in the bedroom has been accessorized with large pillows and a sheepskin rug acting as a relaxed, effortless daybed, as well as a comfy place to sleep at night under the stars.

everyday life as the interior. From the moment the snow thaws in the spring to when the first frost arrives in the fall, the family prefers to wash under the open-sky using the outdoor shower. A sea kayak is at hand for paddles along the nearby coast and a dartboard has been erected on the garage door. However, much of the time is spent taking in the calm atmosphere of the woodland, relaxing on a simple handmade daybed, or listening to the sound of the crashing waves in the distance and, most importantly, spending time together as a family.

Above left: An outdoor shower, naturally screened by foliage, is part of the daily routine at the house. Smooth pebbles from the beach make a practical, mud-free shower floor.

Above: The woodland location ensures an abundant year-round supply of firewood. The wood is kept dry under a simple covered structure in the garden, ready for use on cooler days.

Right: An asymmetric timber garage merges in with the surroundings. The door serves as a useful place to hang a dartboard.
Right, below: The 32-foot (10-meter) square "wagon" holds fond memories for the Brask family and served as the main source of inspiration for the Modern Log House.

WESTWIND ORCHARD

When Italian-Americans Laura, Fabio, and their teenage son, Matteo, first went to see Westwind Orchard in 2002, the land was totally overgrown and bearing little in the way of crops. Even so, the 500 apple trees were in full bloom and the familiar scent and lay of the land reminded them of their childhoods in Italy. Today Laura, a fashion stylist, and Fabio, a photographer, split their time between New York City and the farm in the small hamlet of Accord in the heart of the Hudson River Valley, upstate New York. A farmhouse and converted barn serve as a place to test ingredients for produce sold in the farm store as well as to relax, entertain family and friends, and take in the beautiful views over the Catskill Mountains and Shawangunk Ridge.

At first, the couple planned to live in the pretty stone farmhouse and rent the land to local farmers, but over time they came to love the 32 acres and spent years working the land. Today the farmland boasts over 1,000 trees and produces an abundance of organic apples, Asian and European pears, seedless table grapes, raspberries, blackberries, garlic, onions, herbs, squash, pumpkins, tomatoes, and plums. It is also home to 80 chickens, four Berkshire/Yorkshire pigs, 15 beehives, and their dog, Bosco, an English Labrador.

As one might expect from the charming exterior, the original farmhouse is incredibly cozy. Built in the 1800s by a Dutch family, the low ceilings, exposed hand-hewn beams, and stone walls create a warm, homely feel. The ground floor works in a circular flow around the stairs. The main entrance opens directly into an open-plan dining and sitting room with central stairs leading up to two bedrooms. The kitchen is accessed from either side of the stairs, and a bathroom leads off the kitchen.

The farm has a relaxed, casual vibe, which is reflected in the understated nature of the interior. Laura and Fabio have shunned interior trends in favor of items they truly love. As a result, the home is pared back and simply furnished with a mix of vintage and flea-market finds—often with a modern Danish

Opposite: The pretty stone cottage was one of the factors that drew Laura, Fabio, and Matteo to the farm. A cognac-colored butterfly chair found at a flea market has been draped with a sheepskin throw to serve as a comfy spot to sit and enjoy the peaceful surroundings in the shadow of the Catskill Mountains.

Above: A paint-chipped bench on the terrace outside the front door sets the scene for the welcoming atmosphere of the home.

influence or industrial design—and antiques. Produce from the farm, such as honeycombs, chilies, and corn, can be seen displayed in bowls or in some cases strung from the ceiling, their rich textures and vibrant colors doubling up as both ingredients and decoration. In the compact farmhouse kitchen, an apple ladder rests across the exposed horizontal beams, serving as a simple and effective storage solution for a multitude of kitchen utensils. Braided garlic hangs from a rung, ready to hand, adding an authentic Italian feel to the space.

Functionality reigns supreme in the dining area, which is furnished with purposeful secondhand pieces. The family enjoys meals around a wooden dining table, with seating provided by simple benches. An old dentist's lamp lights up the corner of the room after the sun goes down and a delightful blue antique chest is used for storage. A bell jar containing a fresh honeycomb from the farm sits in the center, waiting to be eaten—the local honeybees forage on apple and vegetable blossom and crops like buckwheat and mustard. Not only

Above: The family has changed little of the original stone cottage, which has served as a farmhouse since the 1800s. Exposed stone walls and a large wooden front door dominate the sitting room and dining room, which have been simply furnished with items collected over many years. **Opposite:** A mid-century black leather rocking chair sits beside a side table from the same era, creating the perfect place to read or simply relax in the natural light from the window. After dark, an old ship's lamp lights up the entrance. Dried flowers from the farm have been informally arranged in a sunny yellow vase, bought at a tag sale in the Hamptons, and placed in the window for a pretty display.

are the crops an invaluable source of food on the farm, but also the raw honey from the beehives is mouthwateringly delicious and a family favorite.

The rich texture and medley of tones in the natural stone wall, original mushroom wood floor, and beams work together to make the sitting room come alive. The relaxed atmosphere owes much to the mismatched furniture. A mid-century rocking chair and side table have been placed beside a bold 1960s rug. The vibrant orange and yellow colors have instant impact, brightening up the cool, dark room and adding an element of coziness. A convenient set of built-in corner shelves creates the perfect spot for much-loved books, and capitalizes on otherwise dead space. The room is lit by a series of industrial lamps sourced at various flea markets over the years.

In the summer the family enjoys lunches alfresco, overlooking the orchard and a magnificent 19th-century English-style barn. Originally used for hay and farm storage, Laura and Fabio worked with architect Kurt Sutherland R.A. in 2006 to transform the barn into a functional studio, creative space, and venue for events and entertaining guests. They salvaged what they could

Above left: Home-grown dried chilies make a vibrant table arrangement, as well as serving as a useful ingredient in recipes.
Above center: Copper pots and pans from a yard sale and a wooden spoon, made by a friend, hang from the rungs of an old apple ladder beside braided garlic from last year's harvest.
Above right: Raw honey from the farm's beehives is ready to be spread on fresh bread using a spoon found on the land. The cone-shaped glass bell jar with its practical wooden base was a thoughtful gift from a friend.
Opposite: The family sits on antique benches around a table found at a flea market for relaxed meals, while a vintage dentist's light provides task lighting. Dried chilies hangs in the window, ready to be used on oven-baked pizzas.
Overleaf: Double glass doors can be opened right up on either side of the barn to allow a lovely breeze to flow straight through. In the distance, a traditional apple orchard ladder is used to gather certified organic apples from one of the orchard's 1,000 trees.

from the original structure. Posts and beams were transformed into the interior structure and cabinets were made from discarded timber. Mushroom wood, which has a lovely silvery finish and which Laura and Fabio were familiar with, having used it on the sitting-room floor, was used to replace the original siding.

The barn was designed to have a light and airy feel. Light floods in through the windows and glass doors and bounces around the open-plan space, which includes a kitchen, dining area, and sitting room. Steps lead up to a mezzanine floor, with a bedroom and bathroom directly over the kitchen. Exposed timber walls create a rustic feel and have been kept deliberately unadorned save for an interesting display in the sitting room. Like the cottage, the space is furnished with an eclectic combination of antique and flea-market finds, handmade pieces, and items picked up on travels. Rugs, blankets, and throws add texture and warmth for a homely feel.

Above: In the barn, a concrete floor juxtaposes with kitchen shelving made from wood for a natural, raw look. The open shelving is laden with mix-and-match pots and pans, glassware, and crockery, emphasizing the relaxed nature of the space.

Opposite: The timber walls, posts, and beams are used as a functional part of the kitchen. An industrial pendant light found in a local antique store hangs from a nail and deer antlers rest on a beam. A cheerful, bright red pitcher found on a work trip to Tennessee adds a pop of color to the kitchen wall.

HERRADURA
Cobram Estate

The couple love to entertain friends and relatives, including Fabio's mother, whose original recipes are used for making delicious jams. The barn is also used to test new products for their home produce, including raw honey, maple syrup, and award-winning preserves. The kitchen has therefore been designed to be as practical as possible. Open shelving, built from salvaged barn wood, keeps items to hand. A bespoke poured cement worksurface matches the rough, raw feel of the room and makes an ideal place to prepare food. An extra-deep stainless steel sink juxtaposes with the wood, its metallic finish catching the light, while under foot the concrete floor has been left bare, save for a small kilim rug in front of the sink.

Laura and Fabio share a mutual love for the beauty and purity of nature and the décor is very much inspired by the countryside around them. A long wooden table built by Fabio bisects the open-plan space. Organic items, such as dried flowers and petrified twigs, have been grouped in a tall black vase and used as an elegant table decoration, alongside a

Above left: The rough edge of a cross-section of tree trunk contrasts with the smoother inner grain, forming a natural tray for a pair of deer antlers.

Above: The golden colors and beautiful texture of dried corn from a previous harvest make a pretty table display.

Opposite: The relaxed, understated dining space reflects the warm and welcoming "come as you are" vibe so commonly found at Italian gatherings. A long dining table has been made using a slab of reclaimed wood and finished with table legs found by a friend in Switzerland. Industrial Tolix chairs are combined with café chairs found in Brooklyn. Overhead, braided garlic from the farm hangs from the ceiling.

handmade chopping board, antlers, and a bowl of dried corn from the farm. Practical, industrial Tolix chairs are mixed and matched with a selection of vintage folding café chairs. A vintage rug found on a trip to Morocco runs the length of the table, clearly defining the dining zone and grounding the space. Its lush texture adds warmth to the entire room.

Magnificent large contemporary pendant lights hang high up in the eaves of the barn. Timber stairs lead up to a snug loft where, as with the rest of the barn, the bedroom is minimal with a delightful mix of pieces. Exposed timber walls create a rich, dramatic backdrop for the modern white headboard, industrial reading

Opposite: The simple, clean lines of the concrete bathroom sink allow the rich textures and color variation in the grains of the timber to dominate. Towels are kept to hand on open shelves and a pretty vase of wildflowers rests on a beam to add a touch of romance.
Above: An antler with colorful wool balls by Brooklyn-based Italian artist Paola Citterio adorns the sitting-room wall. An old sign found in an upstate New York tag sale echoes the colors and traditional primitive style of the arrows that zigzag up the wall between the hand-hewn posts. A swing-arm wall lamp is used for reading.
Right: Darts have been playfully used to pin up Polaroid photos.

lamps, and oil paintings. Across the landing, the bathroom is simply furnished with a concrete sink resting on a cabinet made from repurposed barn wood. The organic and understated decor is in perfect keeping with the minimalist style of the barn and closeness to nature.

As time has passed, Fabio and Laura have become more and more involved in farm life and the local community. Although the 32-acre farm takes a lot of work, the tempo and way of life differ dramatically from their fast-paced city life, giving the pair renewed energy. The family embraces everything the countryside has to offer, from the ripeness of crops at harvest time to the beauty of their decay. Perhaps one day they will move to the farm permanently, but for now though, they love to leave city life behind them at the weekend to relax, play the guitar, gather friends, and get back to their roots.

Above left: A small industrial pendant lamp works well as a convenient reading light in the bedroom. **Above:** The crisp white tone and rounded shape of a Nelson Saucer Pendant Lamp contrast with the exposed timber ceiling, bringing a softness to the harder, straight lines of the overhead structure. **Opposite:** Fresh white linen and a contemporary headboard pop out against the dark timber surrounds. An ethnic-style pillow made from fabric bought from the Hmong tribe on a trip to Cambodia and a 1970s hand-knit blanket from a tag sale add to the cozy feel.

CHAPTER TWO

graphical

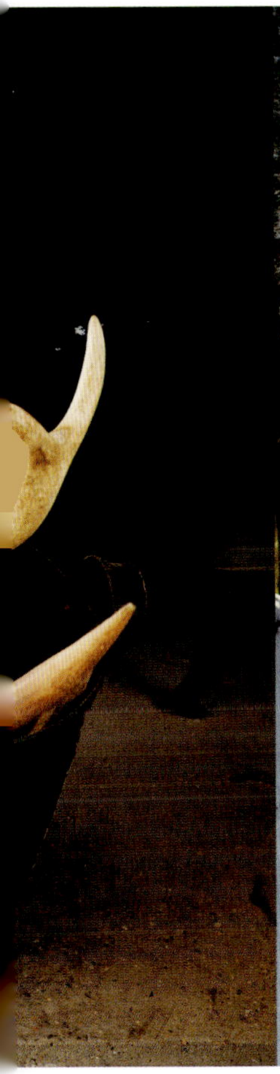

Think clean lines, striking monochrome, and rugged stone surfaces reminiscent of snowy, weatherbeaten landscapes. Graphical homes play with contrast: sharp black and charcoal-colored features are silhouetted by white walls and ceilings. Geometric patterns add interest alongside concrete or weathered wood. The look is softened with warm textures such as cozy sheepskins, cowhide rugs, stacked firewood, and foliage gathered from the surrounding countryside.

WOODLAND VALLEY CABIN

This once derelict hunting cabin in the small hamlet of Phoenicia, in the Catskill region of New York State, has been converted into a magnificent light and airy weekend retreat. Large windows welcome the lush wooded surrounds inside where a carefully curated display of feathers, skulls, and driftwood accentuate the closeness to nature. Crisp monochrome tones and graphic lines juxtapose with warm wood, vintage finds, and treasures from all over the world to create a warm and inviting country home.

The cabin is owned by Amanda Bupp and Bianca Barattini, and it is used as a retreat by family and friends. When they found the property, after a year-long search, the interior of this 1960s hunting lodge was dilapidated and had been vandalized. There was no proper bathroom and the master bedroom was home to a family of squirrels. However, the incredible secluded location, on a lush stand of wooded landscape on Garfield Mountain, combined with its proximity to their everyday lives in New York City, showed the huge potential the old hunting lodge had to become a fabulous weekend get-away.

The exterior has been transformed into a streamlined facade. Wood siding has been stained black and erected with the rough side facing outward for a textured appearance that reflects the rawness of the surrounding nature. The contemporary look of the cabin juxtaposes with the verdant wooded surroundings and looks equally striking all year round—against the backdrop of fresh white snow, the riot of reds in fall, or the vibrant greens in spring and summer months.

Inside, the house was completely gutted before being upgraded into a magnificent light-filled country home. Cut into the hillside, the unassuming front door leads into an entrance hall and snug, which lies directly beneath the bedrooms. A set of stairs leads up to the bulk of the living area, which includes an open-plan kitchen, sitting room, and dining area, which are on the same level as the back garden.

The clean lines of the architecture and monochromatic interior color scheme successfully combine to create a crisp, minimalist feel. An elevated ceiling gives height to the living space and the room is softened by whitewashed horizontal beams. The walls have been painted white throughout, reflecting the natural light—a scarce commodity in wooded areas where the sun is often hiding behind trees. The matt, neutral color also serves as a great gallery wall for the impressive art collection that includes an original limited edition piece by Tracey Emin and a series of prints by Sol LeWitt, and also creates a striking contrast with the linear black furniture used throughout the home.

Previous pages: The large wrap-around deck is perfect for relaxing and entertaining in the summer months. A simple outdoor dining set has been created from a table made with vintage hairpin legs found online and a mix-match of industrial foldaway and modern Plexiglas chairs. When the light fades, the area is lit by the warm glow from a set of string lights.

Opposite: Terraced wood decking leads up to the main entrance and doubles up as a place to store firewood. The door merges into the striking black wood siding of the facade for a clean, modern look, providing a striking contrast with the wooded surroundings of Garfield Mountain.

Above: A simple wheelbarrow is used to carry firewood down the hill to the cabin on cooler days.

Right: An extra-large vintage chopping board doubles up as a tray for a series of cylindrical vessels in black, white, and clear glass, including a Danish design Stelton vacuum jug and a vase filled with ferns from the garden.

Opposite: The light-filled contemporary kitchen is fitted with crisp white cabinets and a pale gray marble that contrasts sharply with the rough texture and darker tones of the wood floor. Statement lighting in the form of a Satellite Chandelier, received as a birthday present, hangs over the space.

The black and white tones and graphical architecture have been softened with texture. Warm wood flooring—salvaged from the rooftop at Soho House in New York—features throughout the home. The unfinished Brazilian ipe boards are known for their hardiness and fire-resistant nature. They also have a beautiful naturally weathered aesthetic with the rich variation in the color echoing the nature outside.

In every room, vast uncovered windows invite the woodland indoors. Skulls, feathers, and driftwood are displayed in vignettes. Sheepskin throws are draped over chairs and across the foot of the bed, instantly making the space more inviting. A large cowhide rug covers the floor in the open-plan living space, adding a touch of coziness, its rounded edges breaking up the crisp lines of the marble hearth extension. The abundance of nature-centric elements adds a tremendous amount of texture and accentuates the feeling of being close to the great outdoors, essentially making the home warm and welcoming.

As with all pared-back homes, the items on display have been thoughtfully edited according to their beauty and the owners' interests at the time, and swapped in and out according to the mood. Treasured ceramics, local vintage and secondhand finds, coffee-table books, and items collected on travels all over the world sit side by side. The result is a captivating variety of objects and a relaxed, personal home.

The kitchen is a highly valued arena, as leisurely weekends allow time for proper cooking and the open-plan nature of the space makes it perfect for entertaining. The fresh, white space has been designed to combine form and function. The sleek cabinets ensure cooking utensils, crockery, and other household items are at hand while neatly hidden from view, while the cabinets have been paired with grout-free honed Carrara marble kitchen tiles for a minimalist, ultra-modern look. Two white industrial-style Tolix stools sit beside the streamlined kitchen island and a statement Satellite Chandelier lights up the area. Greenery, if required, is brought in from the garden to add a fresh touch and a splash of color to the otherwise neutral space. Two small kilim rugs introduce a softer touch to the overall look and feel.

In the winter, the ground is blanketed in snow and the cabin can only be accessed by a four-wheel drive vehicle. Summer pursuits of mountain biking and hiking give way to downhill skiing. In the sitting room, a sofa and armchair are arranged around a fireplace, providing a snug spot to warm up after a day on the slopes. The dramatic black square-shaped fireplace draws the eye, giving the room a strong focal point. Logs are stacked in a long vertical enclave close to the fire, with this elegant storage making a visual impact and adding texture and warmth to the otherwise

Above: The sitting room exudes modern hunting-lodge style. A chair is draped with a sheepskin throw and a white cowhide rug covers the reclaimed wood floor. Contemporary Plexiglas nest tables are in keeping with the strictly monochrome palette.

Opposite: Natural materials play a vital role in adding warmth to the home. Here, a cured piece of driftwood, washed up from the Hudson River in the nearby town of Esopus, adds interest. Stacked wood gives the space added texture and serves as a great backdrop for a peaceful reading corner.

Overleaf, left: Foliage found on the ground in winter sits inside a metal bowl from Calvin Klein Home, for a simple display that reflects the cabin's surroundings.

Overleaf, right: A vintage credenza has been refinished and stained black. Lithographs by Sol LeWitt hang above, the round shapes contrasting with the linear side table. A ceramic pot by good friend Michael Dickey sits alongside a wooden bowl and other treasures.

MINIMALISM AND FASHION
THE SOURCEBOOK OF

clean look. A large cow skull, found on a road trip to Texas, looks out over the room from above the fireplace to complete the modern yet cozy hunting-lodge vibe.

Personal items are neatly squirreled away in a large credenza that sits against one of the living space walls. The long, sleek wooden storage unit was found at a local barn sale and then stained black to give it a new lease on life and to match the monochromatic theme. The surface, partly occupied by a tray of drinks, also provides a great place to display ceramics and treasured hardback books.

At the front of the house, a sizeable master bedroom is flooded with light from three aspects. The windows provide spectacular views of the surrounding scenery, forming a wonderfully peaceful cocoon with the feeling of sleeping high up in the boughs of the trees. An understated square black night table mirrors the shape of the windows, allowing the views to dominate. The natural texture of the Moroccan rugs, leather chair, and a set of built-in wood shelves tempers the strict lines and hard surfaces of the architecture and adds to the country feel of the home.

In the second bedroom, a mid-century bureau has been refurbished and is now used for storage. Above, a poster found in Amanda's parents' attic has been framed and leans against the wall. A geometric patterned rug anchors the room and unifies it with the rest of the living space.

Opposite: The luxurious textures of the soft linen bedding and sheepskin rugs at the foot of the bed create a warm and inviting atmosphere in the master bedroom. The light colors match the calm neutral scheme of the room, allowing the nature outside to dominate the space.

Right: A simple set of open wood shelves break up the stark white walls, adding warmth and texture and serving as a place to display personal items. A Nelson Clock, a decorative bottle found in Africa, and a favorite Fedora are among the objects that are frequently moved around.

In the summer, as much time as possible is spent soaking up the sights and sounds of the surrounding nature first hand. An expansive wrap-around wooden deck cuts into the side of the hill at the back of the house, providing the perfect setting for barbecues. A simple set of folk-inspired string lights has been draped between the house and a nearby tree—perfect when the daylight fades. Vintage pieces, often with an industrial touch, have been upcycled to provide a comfy place to relax.

Two mountain bikes lay in wait, ready for exploring the Catskills or for cycling down to the heart of Phoenicia. However, most of the time is spent unwinding and enjoying the simple life, if only for a few days at a time, soaking up the peacefulness that nature provides before heading back to the hustle and bustle of the city for another busy working week.

Above left: A pillow with a geometric pattern matches the graphical monochromatic theme of the home.

Above: A black-and-white rug, also woven with geometric lines, contrasts with the beautiful, weathered reclaimed flooring.

Opposite: A vintage bureau has been refinished to provide storage. Blankets are kept to hand in a basket in the corner of the room for cooler nights. Cheeseplant leaves have been placed in a vase on the floor to bring a fresh feel to the room.

Augustinerkirche I., Josefsplatz
18 Uhr
19 Uhr
Mittwoch, 1.
Freitag, 3.
November 1967
TOTENGEDENKEN
W. A. MOZART
REQUIEM
Pach
Struve
Clipper
Antalffy
Hölbling
Scholz
Dirigent:
Prof. Julius
Peter

LOMMA COUNTRY HOME

On the site of a dilapidated summer cottage, Susann Larsson and Per Henriksson set about building their dream modern home in the quiet Swedish village of Habo Ljung. Surrounded by trees, and with water on one side and farmland on the other, the contrasting nuances, textures, shapes, and materials of the minimalist interior harmonize effortlessly with the countryside that encircles it.

For interior designer and freelance journalist Susann and entrepreneur Per, it was love at first sight when they found this plot of land in Sweden's southernmost county of Skåne, on the shores of the Öresund, the strait of water that separates Sweden and Denmark.

Susann was immediately drawn to the uncultivated garden with its wood anemones, lily-of-the-valley, honeysuckle, and apple and plum trees. She is a keen gardener and has worked hard to maintain the wild look, planting more of what was already there. The absence of hedges, fences, and other boundaries means you can see right across the flat Skåne countryside, all the way to the cathedral in Lund 8 miles (13 km) away.

The pair tore down the existing structure and set about designing and building a new home together. They chose local architect Ulf Engstrand, excited to find they shared an admiration of the work of Le Corbusier, the Swiss-French

Left: Ivy, cherry tree branches, and a Guiana chestnut have been grouped for their varying heights, shape, and structure, softening the look of the hard concrete behind. The pale pink blossom makes a pretty contrast to the gray and adds a slight Asian feel.
Opposite: Large windows maximize the light in the sitting room, which is especially important during the dark Swedish winters. Plants draw the outside in and create a sense of harmony.

pioneer of modern architecture. Every aspect of the home was designed to combine form and function and require as little maintenance as possible. The walls are made from large, raw concrete blocks, visible on the exterior walls as well as some of the interior walls. The material is incredibly practical and often used in building work due to its inexpensive yet robust qualities. In addition, the concrete provides essential year-round insulation, keeping the house cool in summer months and warm in the freezing winter. The grid-like pattern of the blocks helps to define the graphical look of the home, resulting in a cool, contemporary vibe that makes a striking contrast to the immediate surroundings outside and a magnificent industrial backdrop for the décor indoors.

Susann dislikes feeling trapped indoors, hence the floor-to-ceiling windows on both lower and upper floors. The absence of curtains or shades is common in Scandinavia, where large, unobstructed windows flood interior spaces with natural light—a scarce resource in Sweden during the winter. Here, the windows also allow an uninterrupted view of the garden and surrounding countryside, making the outdoors feel like a natural part of the indoor space.

The main section of the ground floor comprises a cavernous open-plan kitchen, dining area, and sitting room. This serves as a social area where the family can hang out together or entertain friends. The openness also ensures that natural light

Opposite: The primitive geometric lines of a Moroccan Beni Ourain rug work with the graphical nature of the architecture and the lush texture adds a cozy feel to the sitting room.
Above left: The black and white items on the tables are in keeping with the overall monochrome scheme, their round shapes and varying textures creating interest and softening the overall look of the room.
Above: Placing a pretty *Pilea peperomioides* on top of a pile of coffee-table books gives height to a display.
Overleaf left: Round shapes in the form of pots and pebbles help to break up the square feel of the house.
Overleaf right: Built-in wood storage contrasts with the raw cement finish of the fireplace. Trailing ivy and *Pilea peperomioides* add a fresh feel and a pop of color to an otherwise monochrome space and make it come alive.

is generously dispersed. However, the true magic happens when the light hits the inner concrete wall. Depending on the weather, season, and time of day, its color changes. When it's raining, the texture appears dark and creates a brooding atmosphere; when the sun shines, the surface becomes a dazzling white. Throughout the changing seasons, the wall reflects a plethora of colors, the mood of the house altering according to what's happening outside.

Finding a hue to match the concrete walls was no easy feat. Susann finally found the perfect shade of dark gray, which has now been used throughout the home to tie the living areas together. An example of this can be seen in the bespoke kitchen cabinets, which run the length of the room. To match the modern style of the home, the couple opted for a streamlined kitchen

Above left: The organic nature of the wall-mounted wood storage unit contrasts sharply with the plaster walls. Trailing plants break up the horizontal lines and make a pretty feature.

Above: Seasonal flowers have been divided into vases and spread out on a black Asian-style tray to create a pretty centerpiece. Separating flowers in this way allows you to appreciate their individual beauty.

Opposite: The craftsmanship, simple design, clean lines, and round-shaped legs of the classic Hans Wegner Wishbone chairs make them a perfect match with the Jonas Lindvall table "Oak." The wood finish of the table and chairs brings warmth and elegance to the dining area.

Dualit

with a sleek, industrial feel. The rust-free stainless steel surface and easy-to-clean walls were chosen for practicality. Overhead, convenient open shelves span the length of the room and are lined with plants as well as glassware and other kitchen items, the elements grouped according to contrasting textures and forms.

On completion of the home, the concrete and glass facade had a rather heavy feel, so when Susann and Per extended the house to make more room for their teenage children, Harald and Sixten, they added wood panels to soften the look and bring a sense of harmony to the exterior. The same rule has been applied to the interior, with maple-wood flooring covering almost the entire ground and upper floors. The warm wood surface perfectly balances out the steely concrete and adds a Zen feel.

Opposite: The clean lines of the JKE Design kitchen cabinets and shelving work seamlessly with the modern architecture of the house and provide plenty of storage. The rust-free stainless steel surface is a practical choice but it also helps to achieve the industrial look the couple desired.
Above: A shelf runs the length of the kitchen and has been used to display pretty glassware and ceramics, interspersed with more foliage. The plants have been selected for their contrasting leaf shape and structure.
Right: Ivy and *Pilea peperomioides* cuttings have been arranged in an eye-catching display of matching glass vases while waiting to be planted.

Susann and Per's bedroom has a strict gray and white color scheme. A modern Kartell Componibili storage unit doubles up as a practical nightstand, its round shape breaking up the straight lines of the room. Light from two aspects highlights the tonal variation in the plastered walls, the rich colors in the wood floor, and the natural creases in the linen, bringing the room to life.

Opposite: A fluffy sheepskin from the Swedish west coast island of Gotland has been draped over the foot of the bed to create a warm and inviting feel.

In the dining area, the slightly raised dining platform juts out into the garden and is enclosed by glass on three sides. This bathes the area in natural light and creates the feeling of eating alfresco. In winter, cozy sheepskin furs are draped over Danish classic mid-century Hans Wegner Wishbone chairs. The solid wood table and wall-mounted storage unit add a natural element to the space and introduce warmth and softness. The result is a beautifully balanced space in which to enjoy a Swedish "fika" (coffee served with a pastry).

In keeping with the rest of the interior, the comfy living room area has been kept to a strict monochrome scheme. Light colored pillows and a white knit throw contrast with the dark gray L-shaped sofa. Practical nest tables from Hay can be moved around depending on the occasion and how many people are using the space. Underfoot, the graphic pattern of a magnificent Beni Ourain rug, bought on a trip to Morocco, dances with the legs of the table. A side cabinet, painted in Susann's signature dark gray, provides essential storage, resulting in a clean and uncluttered look. It also provides a great platform for treasured items such as books, plants, and ceramics, which bring a personal character to the space.

In this well-insulated home the fireplace wasn't a necessity, but Susann and Per love the coziness it brings to the sitting room. The brick has been plastered over and left raw to work with the adjacent concrete blocks. Bare branches from the garden are placed next to sprays of ivy and Guiana chestnut to create a balance between soft and hard and make the space come alive. Susann uses whatever's available in the garden, including hydrangeas, cherry tree branches, ivy, tulips, and Japanese sea grass. Her artful displays play with contrast in the form of height, color, shape, and texture. The vessels are also carefully chosen, grouping concrete and clay pots with glass vases in different shapes and sizes to create balance. The roundness and texture also cleverly break up and soften the straight lines of the raw concrete blocks.

In warmer months of the year, a glass door from the sitting room is thrown open to create a seamless divide between indoors and outdoors. The covered terrace becomes an extension of the living space, providing a comfy spot to sit and read, socialize, or relax, whatever the weather.

Susann's love of the great outdoors is also evident in the way she incorporates other elements of the surrounding nature into her interior design. An organic shaped pebble from the shore of the Öresund—a mere 330 yards (300 meters) from the home—can be seen on the mantelpiece, an interesting contrast to the raw cement fireplace. A shell-like ceramic pot is displayed on one of the coffee tables. Gray and sand tones associated with the seashore help the home blend into its natural surroundings and introduce elements of the beach.

In keeping with the minimalist theme of the home, the master bedroom is simple and uncluttered. White and gray linen and sheepskin introduce natural elements to the space and

create a peaceful, inviting atmosphere. The varying textures also contrast beautifully with the stark walls to make the room come alive. Round shapes, in the form of a pendant ceiling light and night tables, break up the straight lines and add a contemporary feel.

In the summer the family retreats outdoors and wiles away balmy evenings from the comfort of deckchairs. The fireplace and outdoor heaters on the covered terrace create a cozy outdoor room, and the extra warmth also allows Susann, Per, Harald, and Sixten to enjoy the beauty of the contrasting nature that surrounds them for longer. And with a view like that, who can blame them?

Opposite: A covered terrace serves as an outdoor room in the summer months and somewhere for the family to enjoy the long summer evenings. The natural materials in the wood decking, the round wicker table, and the deck chairs are in keeping with the wild garden. Chunky knit blankets are at hand to keep knees warm after the daylight fades, with the outdoor corner fireplace providing extra heat in colder months.

Above: A greenhouse is used to protect outdoor plants, pots, and paraphernalia from the harsh winter which can reach temperatures as low as 5°F (-15°C).

CHAPTER THREE

homestead

Warming interiors, which bring to mind the soft, muted colors of the autumnal months: horse chestnuts, fallen leaves, a hare bounding over the stubble of harvested fields. Colors are kept to simple neutrals: light and dark browns, creams and milky whites. Whitewashed or limestone walls provide the backdrop for rustic wood furniture, wicker chairs, baskets, and other treasured items. Subtle beiges and off-whites, from freshly laid eggs and dried honeycombs, draw the outside in.

SCANIAN FARMHOUSE

When Gunilla and Sven Montan first set eyes on this traditional 300-year-old farmhouse on a cold January day, it was in total disrepair—no electricity or running water, the original half-timbered clay brick walls were covered in metal sheets, and many of the windows needed replacing. However, the couple could see the potential and have spent years lovingly restoring it to become the wonderful family home it is today.

The magnificent 18th-century farmhouse stands amid open fields in Västra Ljungby, in the county of Skåne in southern Sweden. The Falu red (a dark red paint traditionally used on Swedish cottages and barns), blue, and white home is made up of a cluster of four buildings set around a pretty cobblestone inner courtyard. In winter the wind whistles across the fields and this sheltered yard provides a welcome refuge.

When the pair first bought the farmhouse in 1997, only the north building had been inhabited and the entire space had been left relatively untouched and neglected. The bathroom had a compost toilet and heating was provided by wood-burning

Above: Sheets of metal were removed from the exterior of the original henhouse to reveal beautiful half-timbered walls. The farmhouse exterior was painstakingly renovated using techniques and materials associated with the time when it was built. The blue, white, and red facade represents the traditional colors of rural Scanian homesteads.

Opposite: Replacement timber panels on the south-facing facade were applied in different widths to blend with the existing appearance. A disused chicken coop is still in place on the side of the building.

stoves (which are still used to heat the home today). The other three buildings consisted of a hen house on the south side, a stable on the east side, and a westerly barn—all reminders of the original working farm. The rural location means the property has a beautiful 360-degree vista over fields reaching as far as the eye can see.

Even in the darkness of the Swedish winter, Gunilla, a retired physiotherapist and Sven, a maternity health care consultant, could see its potential. They were enchanted by the original stone floors, wood beam ceilings, and 1920s coal-fired Aga stove. The couple knew that with some tender loving care, this could be a wonderful home and just the renovation project they were after.

At first Gunilla and Sven were tempted to modernize the living space, but were wary this would destroy the charm that initially attracted them. Instead, they set about lovingly renovating the home with the help of local craftsmen, careful to use traditional techniques and natural products such as linseed oil, lime plaster,

Above: Utensils, saucepans, and decorative iron pot stands are kept to hand on a row of hooks in the kitchen. Behind, a slate plate inscribed with a Russian aphorism ("I drank water with a friend, it tasted like wine"), which has been translated into German, was given to the family as a gift.
Opposite: A south-facing conservatory is used to store plants and gardening equipment in winter.
Overleaf: In the summer the extended family gathers around an antique table in the great barn. Mediterranean-style rattan chairs and a kilim rug add warmth to the cold concrete floor and limestone walls of the surrounds. The sense of peace is accentuated by the tremendous ceiling height and views across the flat Scanian farmland.

and paints sympathetic to the era. Today there are still remnants from the farming days—an old sink in the stables has been refashioned into a charming outdoor bathroom, and farming tools still hang in the great barn.

The main challenge was deciding what to remove and what to restore. Anything they decided to replace—including walls, floors, and ceilings, as well as smaller details—was carefully chosen to replicate the original. One of the first things they

Opposite: A pendant light repurposed from a heating lamp used to incubate piglets hangs over the kitchen sink. The sleek porcelain sink, bought on a trip to Shanghai, is flanked by a Portuguese granite and limestone work surface. A Spanish wine jar sits in the window. The trestle table legs have been stained in Falu red to match the exterior of the house.

Above: The textures, materials, and colors were carefully selected to be in keeping with the rustic barn and the heritage of the farmhouse as a whole.

renovated was the facade, replacing broken windows with replica glass panes synonymous with the age of the building. This was a no-brainer for Gunilla, as original glass panes are known to let in a more beautiful and natural light than modern glass. The metal sheets cladding the building were removed to reveal the beautiful original timber frames and clay bricks beneath. It was during this process they discovered that the house held an incredible secret.

Sven noticed one of the timber beams looked older than the others, possibly pre-dating the time of construction. After some research it was discovered that the home had originally been located in a village, but in the 1840s the building was moved to rural Västra Ljungby as part of a land reform, resulting in a larger plot of land and, at the same time, avoiding the risk of fire and the poor hygiene associated with towns at that time. As a result, they were amazed to find parts of the building date back to the 1700s.

Sven and Gunilla have used the home as their primary residence in the past but today it serves as a vacation home, as they prefer the convenience and practicality of a well-insulated apartment in the nearby coastal city of Ängelholm for everyday living. However, the couple were keen for the home to be a welcoming place for their four children—Stefan, Magnus, Carl, and Maria—their partners, and the growing number of grandchildren.

To achieve this, they divided the four sections of the building into individual living areas, each with its own bathroom and kitchen. This means each family has its own private summer house set around a communal inner garden. Gunilla and Sven also gave them free rein on the décor. Fortunately the family shares the same sense of style, preferring to follow their instincts and mix and match old and new rather than sticking to one particular look. As a result, the entire farmhouse is furnished with a beautiful blend of antiques, flea-market finds, heirlooms, modern pieces, items collected on their travels, and even handmade furniture. In Sven and Gunilla's quarter, old drinking vessels collected on overseas trips can be seen

Opposite: A long trestle table built by Sven is large enough to fit the entire extended family in Maria's dining room. A mid-century chair adds a cool contemporary edge to the space and makes an interesting contrast with the brick floor and half-timbered wall. **Above:** A book of pressed flowers curated by Gunilla's father in the 1930s is on display in the home.

hanging in the main entrance. In their living room a jewel-like kilim rug has been placed in front of an original wood-burning stove, which in turn is next to a Swedish antique cabinet.

Maria has installed a freestanding industrial-style IKEA kitchen that creates a great contrast to the floor, which Sven and Gunilla laid using reclaimed, locally made bricks to match the originals. Leading off the kitchen, the dining room houses a comfy mid-century leather chair, a gift from a family friend, and a long trestle dining table handcrafted by Sven, providing enough space for the extended family to eat together on special occasions in fall and winter. The room leads out to the pretty courtyard where they like to eat breakfast in the summer.

Carl's pared-back quarter boasts whitewashed wood-panel walls and ceiling. The bedroom is heated using a vast Danish wood-burning stove, firewood is stored in a basic basket, and a Swedish sheepskin rug lines the floor for a cozy feel. A magnificent 1930s Swedish cabinet is used to store linen and other items.

Opposite: The high ceiling, whitewashed walls, and crisp white bedspread work together to create a peaceful bedroom environment above the barn. Low windows flood the space with light and catch the leaves of the plant on the night table. A subtle floor lamp is used for bedtime reading.
Above: A 1930s cabinet, manufactured in Småland, Sweden, protects neatly folded bed linen and other items from dust. The pillows on the bed pick up the rich, gleaming tones of the birch wood.

Above: Bird-shaped driftwood found on Vancouver Island, Canada in 1992 has been suspended from the rafters.

Opposite: The bespoke white stairs in Carl's quarter were designed by a local carpenter to replicate a chicken ramp. A child safety gate has been added in the same style. The rounded shape of a large black Danish wood-burning stove breaks up the straight lines of the room and makes a magnificent focal point. Perhaps more importantly, it also generates a huge amount of heat, helping to keep the home warm in winter.

In the summer, the entire family loves to gather in the tremendous communal westerly barn where Sven and Gunilla have created a basic rustic summer kitchen. They wanted the kitchen to be functional and flexible enough to cater for everyone. The textures, materials, and colors were carefully selected to be in keeping with the rustic barn and the heritage of the farmhouse as a whole. Comfy rattan chairs surround the large dining table (a family heirloom), creating the perfect space for the family to eat, play games, dance, or simply capture the last of the evening light through the magnificent barn doors.

A few years ago, the couple decided to install a south-facing glass conservatory, leading off the great barn. Not only does the extension provide a place to store plants and gardening equipment in winter, it has also created the perfect spot to enjoy a leisurely coffee overlooking the uninterrupted views of the Skåne countryside, even on the coldest and windiest of days.

Overall, the farmhouse has a natural and relaxed feel, harmonious with the simple lifestyle the family so enjoys when they're here. None of the living areas has any curtains, allowing natural light to pour in through the windows. The space is drafty so shoes are kept on indoors (which goes against Swedish tradition). This also means they share the living area with spiders—something that Gunilla sees as a positive: "It's a sign of a good home—it means it's well ventilated."

The renovations are still ongoing, but the pair try to limit the amount of time they devote to working on the home, preferring to travel or spend time with family. Funnily enough, the uninviting darkness, which initially made the home feel so unappealing on that cold January day, has become one of the greatest things about the house. The rural location means it's silent, except for birds, the wind racing across the fields, and children laughing in the garden; and it also becomes pitch black at night. These are rare commodities in this day and age. The beautiful farmhouse has become a welcoming refuge and somewhere the family can truly switch off from daily modern life.

THE HILL IN VERMONT

True isolation is a rarity in this day and age. Yet, high on a hill top, amidst 100 acres of luscious New England pasture shared with black bears, coyotes, wild deer, and an array of beautiful birds, is the Dole family home. "The Hill" farmhouse is simply furnished with a mixture of antiques, handmade items, vintage finds, and wonderful pieces of art. Natural materials and a neutral color scheme unify the eclectic pieces and work in harmony with the surroundings. The result is a peaceful home for Nadia, Kevin, and their daughter, Poet.

This remote farmhouse in Bennington, Vermont is located on the very top of a hill at the end of a long dirt track, any sign of civilization long since fallen away. The high altitude affords breathtaking views over open fields toward four mountain ranges in New York, New Hampshire, Vermont, and Connecticut. Nadia Dole, photographer and stylist, as well as owner of a café, wholefoods market, orchard, and farm store, and husband Kevin had always dreamed of living on the farm. Six years ago the property became available to rent, so on a cold winter's day the couple strapped on their snow shoes and trudged up the hill through the snow to view it. The beautiful yet modest space is now also home to four-year-old Poet and long-term guests from all over the world.

Above: The rich textures and dark color of the timber farmhouse contrast with the lush green fields and blue haze of the mountains behind. A chicken coop is conveniently placed a short distance from the house.

Above right: Tolstoy, a Percheron-Friesian draft horse, and Splash, a Quarter Horse, graze on the fresh pastures in front of the house.

The farmhouse was built using wood salvaged from a former five-story apple barn originally situated across the track from where "The Hill" now stands. In 1970 the old barn was carefully demolished and gradually re-constructed into its present form. These days, the 100 acres of farmland is home to horses, dogs, cats, and over 40 ducks and chickens. When not tending to the farm, the family enjoys long walks through the fields, gathering wild flowers for the house or foraging for food.

Inside, little of the simple rustic structure has been changed since the Dole family took up residence. Although it appears compact from the outside, the farmhouse is deceptively spacious and comprises three floors. On the ground floor, an open-plan space, arranged in a horseshoe shape, contains two sitting rooms, dining area, and kitchen. The original wooden walls and simple exposed beam structure—remnants from the apple barn—dominate the living area. The horizontal beams create an illusion of width, visually enlarging the room, resulting in a surprisingly cavernous living space.

Nadia's design philosophy is straightforward: simple and natural, but with a sense of purpose. Her home has been minimally furnished with an eclectic array of items, collected from different eras, styles, and countries as far away as France and Tibet. Antique and vintage finds sit side by side with handmade pieces and wonderful works of art. Overhead, 1920s schoolhouse pendant lamps light up the living area. The neutral color palette of creams and muted tones serves to unify the disparate items for a pared-back, fuss-free look. Natural fabrics, such as linen and cotton, have been draped over furniture or turned into pillow covers, brightening up the space while adding comfort.

Previous pages: The single-glazed windows open inward and upward with dramatic results. Light pours in, highlighting the beautiful structural ceiling and the grooves in the wood floor. A cool breeze flows through the house. In late fall, they are replaced with storm windows.

Above left: A row of linen aprons in muted tones makes a delightful display on the back wall. Vintage rolling pins are stored in the pockets.

Opposite: The kitchen is simple yet purposeful and made entirely from salvaged items. The timber wall has aged gracefully over time, the color variation creating a dramatic backdrop. An industrial unit with antique bin pull handles has been repurposed into charming kitchen cabinetry.

BREAD
&
PUPPET

Above: Fresh eggs from the chicken coop and duck house are one of the simple pleasures of " The Hill". Eggs from the endangered Cayuga ducks, which are almost black in the cooler months and a pale blue-gray in the summer, are arranged alongside the cream and brown eggs from the hens, making a lovely display.
Above right: The beautiful patina and detail on the Polynesian prayer altar in the kitchen.

Opposite, left: A row of pottery in different shapes and sizes, made by Nadia, lines the kitchen windowsill. Wild flowers are interchanged with cut herbs, the beauty of their shape accentuated by the backlight from the window.
Opposite, right: A rustic stool with chipped paint is used as a plinth to display daisies and pebbles found on the land.

On warm days, large windows salvaged from the apple barn lift inward and upward, dramatically suspended from the ceilings by chains, allowing the breeze to keep the house cool and well ventilated. These openings emphasize the panoramic vistas over the breathtaking New England countryside, punctuated only by passing wildlife. At sunrise the home springs to life, the shades of the inner walls moving through a multitude of pinks, oranges, and fiery reds. At night, the sky is filled with a thousand stars, and the fields magically glow with the twinkling light from dancing fireflies.

In fall and winter the house is heated using a modern wood-burning stove in the living room, and a comfy chaise longue and sofa have been arranged to enjoy the warmth and homely feel of the fire. Simple white slipcovers have been thrown over the seating to give them a new lease on life and create a cozy corner for Nadia, Kevin, and Poet to listen to records on a turntable, play musical instruments, or read. Nadia is a keen seamstress and many of the natural linen pillow covers have been hand sewn, using fabric from her own store. Natural linen has a forgiving nature and gets softer the more it's washed. The breathable texture also means it stays cool to the touch in summer, and the fresh fabric adds a lightness to the room.

The home is adorned with oil paintings, giving the space a unique personality. Nadia, an avid art collector, scours secondhand stores and antique fairs for new works, often stumbling across exciting finds in the most unexpected places.

Her home is full of bold still lifes and fascinating portraits. Over the side table in the sitting room hangs a male portrait discovered in a secondhand store in Rhode Island. Amazingly, Nadia knew the sitter.

The farmhouse kitchen has a simple, rustic feel. Open shelves have been made from reclaimed wood and wall-mounted using Victorian antique cast-iron brackets. The shelves are lined with an array of pottery that has been collected or made by Nadia and fired in her kiln in the basement. The cups, bowls, and pitchers are mostly white or natural with wonderful textures—sometimes a result of glazing mishaps. These items, mixed in with antique copper pieces collected on travels abroad and other useful kitchen items, stand out against the wood-paneled wall.

A striking Polynesian prayer altar, found upturned on the floor of a Boston warehouse, has been repurposed as a kitchen island. Nadia spends a lot of time in the kitchen, preparing family meals or experimenting for her café menu and photography workshops. She cooks with whatever is to hand, preferring to use the fresh flavors of local ingredients when they are in season. Family feasts are enjoyed in the basic, pared-back dining area. Light floods the space from two aspects, giving the illusion of eating alfresco. Glasses and napkins are kept to hand in a cabinet, which was a wedding present from Nadia's grandmother. On the facing wall, a tall glass-fronted hutch, which came with the house, showcases ceramics, vases, and other treasures.

In the entry hall modern storage has been shunned in favor of a delightful green armoire. The couple ordered the bespoke piece from a well-known cabinet-maker, and the design was inspired by a French armoire Nadia recalled seeing as a child. Next to this, a simple wooden bench doubles up as a place to store firewood.

Upstairs, the rooms are tucked into the roof space and all have sloping ceilings. As well as the master bedroom, there is an open-plan area furnished with a desk and daybed, plus another bed for the family's frequent guests.

Meals and afternoon tea are enjoyed at a 19th-century pine harvest dining table purchased 25 years ago in Montreal for Nadia's first apartment. The natural woven seating of the dining chairs is slowly coming unraveled, enhancing the relaxed nature of the home.

Opposite: A bunch of daisies has been arranged in a white pitcher for a simple but pretty display, helping to draw the outside in.

The farmhouse's sole bathroom is charmingly simple. Cross light from an undressed window highlights the variety of natural colors, patterns, and rich textures in the wood-paneled walls, making the raw material come to life. As a result the room has a warm cabin-like feel. A salvaged lath-cladded accent wall breaks up the wider planks and provides a perfect backdrop for an antique mirror and reclaimed porcelain sink. The recycled building material echoes the grayish tints in a rustic bathroom cabinet, made at the same time as the house. A freestanding cast-iron roll-top bath, found at auction, provides a touch of luxury to the otherwise Spartan space. The classic double-sided shape matches the simplicity of the room, while the decorative lion-claw feet add a rather fanciful, feminine touch. A shower curtain is drawn across to create a sanctuary, shared only with chickens, ducks, wild deer, and black bears outside the window.

Above left: Nadia collects art from all over the world. The nude portrait was found in a *brocante* (a secondhand market), in Maussane, France. Beneath, a gray chair has been painted in the same shade as the folding table, found at auction on a visit to Cape Cod.
Above: Dried honeycombs found in the garden in winter make an interesting year-round display.
Opposite: A Kasanof's & Paramount Bakeries tin bought in an antique store in Boston over 20 years ago sits above the green armoire. The impressive "Blueberry" painting is by John Young.

KASANOF'S & PARAMO
BAKERIES

"The Hill" is a truly magical home. The ethereal feel of the interior and the basic, natural materials work in total harmony with the spectacular countryside. The creative life of the family is completely in tune with the environment and a living reality of an idealized version of country life that many aspire to. Guests come and go throughout the year, making the dwelling as transient as the migratory wildlife and changing seasons outside the windows.

Previous pages: The curved shape and decorative touches on an ornate mirror and rounded porcelain sink juxtapose with the rough texture and straight lines of the lath-cladded wall. An old schoolhouse light hangs above the mirror, while a floaty shower curtain brings a softness to the otherwise rustic, raw nature of the space.

Above left: The farm's chickens and ducks lay around a dozen eggs a day. The coop is positioned near the back door for convenience.

Above: A hammock hung between trees in the front garden provides a shaded place in which to relax.

Opposite: The covered porch in the farmhouse entrance doubles up as a place to store tools. Nadia's and Poet's boots await a long walk.

CHAPTER FOUR

waterside

It is the play of light dancing on the surface of the water that makes lakes, streams, and oceans so fascinating. Homes decorated in tones of cool white, grays, and soft shades of blue reflect the ever-changing nature of water. Rough textures such as raw slate, concrete, and reclaimed wood contrast with accessories made from rattan, cotton, and wool, bringing the space to life and creating an oasis of comfort and calm.

LAKESIDE RETREAT

The Lakeside Retreat nestles quietly on the north shore of Lake Furesø, on the Danish island of Zealand, and is accessed via a mud track and a set of steep steps, or alternatively, and possibly more romantically, by boat. Completely hidden from view, the wood cabin is just 200 feet (60 meters) square, but what it lacks in size is made up for in a beautiful open-plan living space and magnificent vistas of the lake. In fact, the cabin is so private, remote, and peaceful it's hard to believe it's a short 25-minute drive from the hustle and bustle of the Danish capital, Copenhagen. It is this tranquility that drew Per Henriksen, his girlfriend, and their dog to this idyllic weekend retreat.

Per, owner of Copenhagen's vintage watch store Franz Jaeger & Me, had been looking for somewhere to escape from hectic city life at the weekends and during the summer months. When he first saw the little black-and-white cabin in 2011, he recalls looking out over the lake and feeling an immediate sense of calm. The house was over budget and needed a tremendous amount of work, but it provided just the solitude and peace he longed for.

Built in 1939 by a grocery-store owner, the ground floor of The Lakeside Retreat comprised a warren of small rooms, giving it a rather dark, pokey feel. The roof needed replacing and a lot of the wooden structure was rotten. Per was keen to turn the space into somewhere he and his girlfriend could feel

Opposite: The modest black-and-white retreat is situated directly on the shores of Lake Furesø. The spacious pontoon-style decking stretches out beyond the shoreline, creating a sense of living on the water.

Above left: An outdoor corner sofa by Tripp Trapp serves as a comfy place to read, nap, socialize, or even sleep beneath the stars when weather permits. After sunset the whole area is lit with lanterns.

Above: In warmer months the indoor bathroom is exchanged for soaks in a contemporary Firenze bathtub under the open sky. The rounded egg shape breaks up the straight lines of the architecture of the cabin.

comfortable throughout the year, surrounded by items they love. Although he had a good idea of the style he was after, he sought room layout advice from friend and owner of Danish store Rue Verte, Michala Jessen.

Per set about reconfiguring the existing space, digging down 3 feet (1 meter), knocking down walls, and re-wiring and insulating the entire house. During the renovation he was intrigued to find the walls had originally been insulated using old bottling and packaging materials and wooden crates from the previous owner's grocery store, as well as newspapers dating back to 1939, the year the house was built. The excavation also uncovered the remains of a fox, whose skull can now be seen displayed in the sitting room.

Today the ground floor is made up of an entrance hall and bathroom and one large, open-plan space comprising a kitchen, dining area, and living room. Large double doors open out onto the deck, allowing a warm breeze to float in during the summer months. Just off the living area, separated by a set of glass doors, is the guest room. An oak "volcano" floor ties the entire space together, so-called

Above left: A small bay with a gently sloping shoreline provides an ideal place to launch a canoe or stand-up paddleboard.
Above: The surface of the lake shimmers with a mesmerizing plethora of colors depending on the light. In the late afternoons the water appears almost white, broken up by the reflections of the boughs of a tree.
Opposite: A pair of sunbeds from Tripp Trapp sit side by side on the natural sandy beach. A simple wooden crate has been used as a table on which to place drinks, books, and essentials. After sundown, the beach is lit with candles for a romantic evening under the stars.

Above: A set of café chairs is paired with a lightweight table on the corner of the deck, for alfresco meals surrounded by water. The light, foldable nature of the furniture makes it easy to store in winter. The table has been decorated with a Finnish design candelabra, glass votive holders, and pots of tall grass, reflecting the reeds in the shallows of the lake.

Opposite: An over-sized military light and its tripod stand make a statement on the corner of the outdoor terrace, contrasting with the natural surroundings for a quirky way to light the area at night.

for its beautiful burnt effect finish. The wooden floor was carefully chosen to be able to withstand the expansion and contraction that comes with living close to the water, and for its raw, natural appeal.

The changing scenery of the lake can be seen from every room in the house and the windows flood the rooms with light that reflects off the water, the colors and atmosphere of the home changing with the weather. In the summer, the huge outdoor terrace and beach serve as wonderful outdoor rooms and the windows and doors are thrown open to let in the sights and sounds of the great outdoors, resulting in a smooth transition between inside and out.

The home adheres to a minimalist style, yet it boasts modern comforts such as a state-of-the-art coffee machine, French range stove, and streamlined kitchen cabinets. Despite this, Per has veered away from an entirely contemporary look, preferring to furnish the space with items from different eras and parts of the world. Antique Chinese furniture, African artifacts, flea-market finds, and gifts from friends sit beside designer pieces and Danish works of art.

The clean monochrome tones of the kitchen are softened by warm, natural textures from wooden utensils, chopping boards, plants, and a rattan basket. The stainless steel of the work surfaces has been replaced with a wooden side panel to create a seamless transition between the cabinets and the wooden floor.

The interior accents of earthy blues, grays, greens, and browns imitate the surrounding wilderness, picking out colors from the lake, its bank, and ancient beech trees that flank the house. Fresh flowers arranged in antique Chinese clay pots in the dining area and sitting room are in keeping with flowers that grow naturally in the area, and provide the only real pop of color—a vibrant fuchsia pink—which creates a striking contrast with the stark white walls.

Textures play a big role in the décor—velvet, silk, suede, cotton, and wool sit side-by-side to speak to the senses and create a cozy atmosphere. In the kitchen, an industrial stainless steel work surface has been combined with high-gloss kitchen cabinets fitted with rubber handles for a natural touch. For a spot of fun, the handle on the fridge door has been replaced with a quirky brass bull's head. In stark contrast to the sleek kitchen, a paint-chipped antique Chinese cabinet is used to store glassware, napkins, and other kitchen items. This beautiful piece, picked up in a store on Zealand, adds a rawness to the space

Opposite: Per likes to play with textures throughout the home. In the dining area, a collection of limited edition black handmade ceramics by K. H. Würtz subtly contrast with the smooth surface of the B&B Italia table.
Above left: Olive oil, vinegar, and seasoning are to hand on a simple wooden tray next to a Lacanche range stove. Light catches the leaves of fresh basil and flowering lavender, adding a vibrant splash of color to the back wall.
Above: A copper bowl and vase of flowers sit alongside a geometric black sculpture by Danish artist Peter Bonnen in the entranceway.

and also creates the perfect place to display natural treasures, such as Per's skull collection, antlers, and a vase of feathers. A magnificent painting of a skull by Christian Lemmerz hangs over the cabinet to complete the fascinating animal-themed vignette.

In the dining area, chairs from Rue Verte have been upholstered in tactile petroleum velvet. The soft, lavish texture of the chairs, combined with the round shape of the Italian-made dining table, introduces a touch of luxury and breaks up the clean lines and hard surfaces of the kitchen, adding harmony and balance.

In fall and winter (or on cooler spring and summer days) the couple like to relax on a sumptuous L-shaped sofa and read, catch up, or take in the views of the lake through the window. The round coffee table and curved lamp help to break up the square shape of the room, while the statement Adnet Gubi mirror bounces light around the room. Another antique Chinese

Above left: The old unrestored paint surface of an antique Chinese cabinet reveals the raw wooden structure beneath, adding to its charm.
Above: Arranging similarly colored items like feathers and branches in a vase makes an interesting replacement for fresh flowers. It's also a great way to bring nature indoors.
Opposite: An antique Chinese cabinet forms the basis of a brown-and-black themed vignette in the kitchen. Fox and ape skulls are joined by a third skull in the form of a painting. An old and extremely heavy African figurine, thought to have been lying on the ground for many years in the Congo, stands on the floor beside the cabinet and a black sheep skin rug lies on the floor.
Overleaf: A comfy dark blue L-shaped sofa from CasaShop in Copenhagen dominates the sitting room. Circular objects, in the form of a mirror, coffee table, lamp, and an African wagon wheel, add to the softness of the space. A brown pillow picks up the colors in a painting by Thomas Øvlisen.

Above: Old fencing masks found at auction in Sweden decorate the slate chimneybreast.

Opposite: The cabin is heated with a wood-burning stove cut into a slate-clad surround. The floor-to-ceiling natural stone finish brings the feeling of the outdoors into the sitting room and adds texture, making the wall come alive. Velvet curtains can be pulled across the bottom of the stairs to cordon off the bedroom for privacy.

side cabinet, formerly used to store rice, runs the length of the wall, mirroring the one in the far corner for balance and providing the perfect place for a well-stocked bar! A cozy wood-burning stove provides the only source of heating, but it is enough for the entire cabin. The chimneybreast is specially designed to heat up and retain warmth.

A steep set of stairs lead up the side of the chimneybreast to the main bedroom. The small turret-like room has been enlarged to accommodate a double bed. The windows on three sides have been left curtain-free to flood the space with light, and the panoramic views of the lake generate the feeling that you're sleeping in a lighthouse, and at the same time provide a calm oasis in which to start the day.

In the summer months as much time as possible is spent outside. Weather permitting, the pair spend their days out on the lake, making use of the motor boat or canoe, or they simply take in the scenery from the comfort of an outdoor sofa on the large wooden lake-side terrace, enjoying the water lapping on the deck and the warm breeze coming off the water. An outdoor bathroom provides the perfect spot for a morning shower or bath after a dip in the lake.

Barbecue lunches are enjoyed on a dining table overlooking the water. The table was chosen for both form and function. Made from lightweight concrete, the rough finish fits in with the surrounding nature, and the material makes it easy to move around. The table is simply decorated with flea-market purchases, items picked up in Copenhagen, and foliage from the garden, all in muted tones to allow the view of the lake to steal the show.

As dusk falls, the deck is lit with the warm glow of candlelight from the many lanterns dotted around. Vast ex-military lamps, bought at auction, add a cool industrial feel to the space and have been especially adapted to illuminate the water, but the best place to enjoy the romantic ambience is sitting by the log fire on the beach, with the lights of Copenhagen twinkling far away in the distance.

HUDSON FARMHOUSE

In upstate New York, a 19th-century farmhouse in the heart of scenic Hudson Valley serves as an idyllic retreat for the Billinge family. Muted gray and cream tones combine with original wood flooring and salvaged wood-paneled walls to create a rich, natural palette throughout. Simply furnished using handmade furniture and vintage finds, the newly renovated warm and inviting vacation home reflects both its past and the serene landscape in which it lies.

Known locally as "The Cottage," the white-clapboard farmhouse is one of a cluster of houses in the small village of Freehold. Debby and Simon Billinge, together with their children, Ian, Sophie, and Isabel, were immediately taken with the home, historically the "poor cousin's house" on what was once a large family estate. Outside, there is a charming garden, a barn, an outhouse, and a pond shared by an abundance of wildlife including chipmunks, snakes, toads, wild deer, and birds. The magnificent view from the wrap-around porch looks out over a stone wall and a white picket fence toward undulating hills and land.

The house itself is a mixture of disparate parts resulting from a variety of extensions and adjustments over the years. Today, the ground floor works in a circular flow. The entry hall has three exits, with the choice of going left into the dining room or right into the sitting room or up the staircase opposite. The south-facing

Left: An old red barn, used for fun games of table tennis and for storage, overlooks the pond in the farmhouse grounds.
Opposite: The mix of old and new windows and extensions from different eras were some of the factors that first attracted the Billinge family to the house. They appreciated the scale of the home and the private garden, a direct contrast to their rather cramped apartment in New York City.

dining room occupies the oldest part of the house, thought to date back to the 1860s. This leads through to a sunroom, which is a more modern extension and contains the second sitting room, which in turn leads into the north-facing kitchen. From there, the main sitting room completes the loop. The upstairs comprises four bedrooms and a bathroom.

Despite the disjointed feel, the Billinges were drawn to the creaking floorboards and inconsistent fittings (every room on the ground floor has a different style of window), and also the magnificent natural light. They instinctively knew the house could be turned into a sanctuary in which they could spread out, cook, entertain, and relax on weekends and vacations—the perfect antidote to their cramped year-round living space in New York's Brooklyn.

Tara Mangini and Percy Bright of Jersey Ice Cream Company were entrusted to design, renovate, and furnish the home. The goal was to create a more unified interior while being careful to maintain the building's heritage, accentuating the original features that had so graciously drawn the family to the house in the first place.

Left: A handmade storage cabinet doubles up as an outdoor table on the wrap-around terrace. The unfinished paintwork reflects the informal feel of the house and garden.
Opposite: The family relaxes on rattan chairs on the porch while gazing out over the undulating hills of the Hudson Valley. To combat chilly evenings, blankets are conveniently placed in a nearby basket. The wooden floor has been painted pale gray to match the white and gray exterior of the house.
Overleaf, left: A dining table made from old floorboards has been coupled with disparate vintage chairs, echoing the relaxed atmosphere of the house. An industrial-style light system, made from lath and a row of filament light bulbs, hangs over the table.
Overleaf, right: Plates, napkins, and silverware are all to hand in a glass-fronted bespoke side cabinet made from lath. The drawing of "The Cottage" was left behind by the previous owners.

A simple color palette of soothing muted grays and creams were selected to create a light-hearted feel and reflect the serenity of the surrounding nature. The calm colors also provide a welcoming respite from the powerful visual stimulation of big city life, helping the Billinges to unwind quickly on arrival.

Throughout, the walls and ceilings have a light gray tone. This simple plaster finish is an age-old material that has recently seen a popular resurgence. Not only is it durable, but it also has a raw texture that complements the simple feel of the house. When light hits the surface, it draws out the natural variation in the color, adding a sense of depth.

Layers of laminate, cheap wood flooring, and old brown carpet have been stripped away to reveal the original wood floor, giving rooms a natural, organic touch. Windows have been simply dressed with hand-sewn silk curtains, with the sheer fabric adding a delicate touch to each room and letting in soft pools of natural light to give an airy feel. Despite this unity, every room delivers a delightful element of surprise and individuality, in some cases drawing on reclaimed items from the valley, in others cleverly revealing more of the building's past.

The north-facing kitchen has been predominantly designed for functionality: light floods the room from two aspects—over the sink and from a skylight. The hardy butcher-block work surfaces are designed to maximize workspace and provide a practical food preparation area for a family of keen cooks. The kitchen

Above: Sofas found on Craig's List are arranged in an L-shape around a handmade coffee table. They are strewn with pillows embroidered with flowers and insects from Coral & Tusk in Brooklyn, reflecting the nature outside. A fluffy shag pile rug anchors the space and adds warmth.
Opposite: The essence of the garden room is enhanced by an unframed painting found in a thrift store and a large indoor plant. Pillows, a throw, and a sheepskin rug create a snug corner for a quiet read.

Overleaf, left: The farmhouse kitchen is fitted with a large vintage sink salvaged from a flower store, which has been custom-built into the existing cabinets. Flowers from the garden rest on the windowsill, adding to the romantic feel of the room.
Overleaf, right: A paneled door leading to the adjoining mudroom has been painted in the same dual-tone colors as the kitchen, with striking results.

PLENTY MORE

GARDENDESIGNDETAILS arne maynard
NATURAL GARDEN
Planting the Natural Garden
Gardens with Atmosphere Arne Maynard with Sue Seddon

cabinets are handmade, with some of the drawers repurposed from discarded materials from the previous fitments. The cabinets hide more unsightly items such as the fridge, oven, and pots and pans for a fuss-free look.

The real show-stopper here is the striking dual-toned wall. Half light gray plaster and half dark blue Benjamin Moore paint, the wall is a wonderfully fresh take on classic wainscoting and the crisp dividing line is a modern replacement for a dado rail. Not only does the bold blue hue add drama and a rather romantic touch to the room, it also provides a great backdrop for the statement vintage sink, countertops, kitchen utensils, and vintage copper pots. The contrasting lighter shade above the dark adds visual height and dimension to the room while breaking up the look to prevent it becoming overbearing.

Above left: The rich texture and color variation in a ceramic sink, found at secondhand store ReStore, works beautifully with the rough surface of the wooden cabinet.

Above: A handmade wall-mounted wooden shelving unit is used to display books and a vase containing a single flower from the garden. A simple filament light bulb hangs from the ceiling, emphasizing the understated nature of the home.

Opposite: Timber from an old barn has been used to create practical bathroom furniture, including a rustic sink unit and bathroom cabinet.

SOAP

Layers of wall covering in the master bedroom were peeled back to reveal decorative wallpaper from years gone by. Swatches are exposed in patches around the room to celebrate the heritage of the home, while the floral bedspread and vintage accessories emphasize the romantic nature of the room.

Opposite: Many of the items in the bedroom, including the bed frame, nightstand, and headboard, have been made by hand from reclaimed wood, adding to the rustic feel of the home.

In contrast, the dining room is a somewhat calmer place, with the wonderful original glass windows looking out over the gentle undulating hills. Although south facing, it's kept cool by the eaves of the wrap-around porch. Most of the furniture is handmade, including a long dining table designed to host large dinner parties or lavish family breakfasts, a glass and wood-sided cabinet, and an industrial-style strip of lighting over the table. A lighter shade of gray has been used in a band around the top of the room and on the ceiling to give an illusion of height. The lower darker shade makes a magnificent backdrop for wildflowers brought in from the garden. In the evenings, the candlelight dances with the textures, bringing the room to life.

At the back of the house a sunroom provides a perfect spot to relax and simply enjoy the beautiful landscape. The A-frame ceiling and accent wall have been dramatically clad with wood from a local disused barn that was purchased with the sole purpose of making items for the home. The panels have been whitewashed to achieve a gray tone and blend with the pigmented plaster. Even so, no two planks are the same, making the lumber a wonderfully decorative material and giving the space an organic yet cozy and warm feel. The room has been simply furnished with snug vintage sofas and a basic handmade coffee table.

Upstairs, a once dark and pokey room has been transformed into a lofty, light-filled master bedroom. Dilapidated wood flooring has been given a new lease on life with a lick of paint and a low-slung ceiling has been knocked through to expose an A-frame roof. During the replastering, pretty wallpaper was discovered under layers of other wallcoverings and has been left exposed in patches around the room. The extra ceiling height, combined with the light colored floor and statement walls, creates an almost fairytale-like atmosphere. The room has been entirely furnished using reclaimed items, including a headboard made from a screen door, two nightstands, and a chest of drawers in keeping with the pared-back nature of the farmhouse.

Across the landing, a second bedroom has been transformed by way of a statement lath accent wall. The rich composition and warm tones of the inexpensive, often discarded material has given the otherwise neutral room a warm, rustic ambience. The painted wood floor and secondhand pale-colored rug give the entire space a light visual lift. A simple stool is used as a night table.

The smaller, third bedroom has been fitted with a remarkable handmade wood bed frame and headboard with space-saving built-in drawers for storage. The country feel has been offset by the walls which have been artfully decorated with hundreds of hand-painted pale blue polka dots, while floral print bed linen accentuates the romantic look and feel of the room. Simple wall-mounted wood shelving is used to display a much-loved collection of books and other treasures.

At the back of the house, an upstairs family bathroom has been given a revamp using simple materials. An off-white textured ceramic sink sits atop a cabinet made from the same salvaged barn wood seen in the sunroom. The walls have been decorated using tadelakt, a natural lime-based plaster from Morocco, known for its decorative and waterproof qualities. The natural materials and fresh light colors create a spa-like feel and a perfect sanctuary in which to unwind.

It's no wonder that on the drive up from New York City, the Billinge family feels an immense sense of excitement at the prospect of spending time at the home, whether relaxing in the garden, jogging to the local swimming hole, or long evenings on the porch surrounded by nature. Often, they go to bed early, unaccustomed to the lack of streetlights and noise. Debby harbors the dream to turn part of the residence into a small flower farm or nursery one day but for now, the family just comes to enjoy the tranquility of the place, the full moon through the kitchen skylight, or magical fireflies lighting up the garden with a thousand twinkling stars at night.

Above: A handmade rustic headboard conveniently doubles up as shelving for books and other treasured items. The rich color variation in the wood adds texture to the bedroom.

Opposite: Neatly arranged blue-and-white themed pillows—a mixture of vintage and chain-store finds—match the color of the floral bedspread and a wooden stool found on Etsy for a coherent look.

SUMMER COTTAGE

Cold, dark, snowy Scandinavian winters give way to long hours of sunlight, green pastures, and sparkling seas. Summer vacations are spent in the great outdoors, soaking up the warm rays, bathing, relaxing, hiking, cooking from scratch, and spending time together as a family. Like many Danes, retirees Else and Keld Jorgensen head to their charming traditional summer cottage in the pretty village of Tisvildeleje, on the north coast of Zealand. Often joined by their children and grandchildren, the family lead a back-to-basics lifestyle in the cozy, understated living space and garden, making the most of the abundance of natural light.

When Else and Keld first went to see the cottage in 2003, they were drawn to its proximity to the white sands and soft dunes of the nearby beach on the shores of the Kattegat Sea, a mere five-minute walk from the house. They loved the traditional style of the cottage, with its easily manageable 600 square feet (55 square meters) of open-plan living space and large garden and its promise of plenty of time alfresco. The property is built on farmland, sold off by a local farmer in 1961 to make way for summer residences. The exterior is stained in Falu red, a Swedish dye used in a red paint, frequently used on wooden structures such as cottages and barns. Deer antlers adorn the front of the house as decoration and as a reminder of the

Left: The colors of white sands and sparkling blue seas have inspired the interior decoration of the cottage.

Opposite: Else and Keld's traditional Danish summer cottage is designed for enjoying the outdoor life to the full. The large wrap-around wooden deck serves as an extension of the living space, offering two different seating options, depending on where the sun is.

farmland on which the cottage resides. Today, the garden is filled with the scent of roses, climbing clematis, and a variety of trees, and there is a large lawn where the children can play. A spacious L-shaped wrap-around deck creates the perfect spot for long lunches or a freshly brewed afternoon coffee.

A gate opens on to a garden path leading up to the cottage door. Inside, just off the narrow entry hall, is a bathroom, with the main room straight ahead. This large open-plan space includes the kitchen, dining area, and sitting room. Two bedrooms flank the room at each end. There is also an annexe in the garden with a third bedroom, a convenient and quiet place for Else and Keld to sleep when the whole family comes to stay.

Above left: Bicycles, an ever-popular method of transport in Denmark, are stored in a basic wooden shelter in the garden.

Above: A smart wood shed provides a convenient space to store firewood all year round. The Falu red stain and small-scale white-framed window perfectly match the exterior of the cottage for a uniform look.

Opposite: A small annexe in the corner of the garden, also exhibiting the red and white colors of the house, provides extra living space and a peaceful place to sleep when extra guests arrive.

The cottage is deliberately simple, understated, and relaxed. True to classic Scandinavian style, the walls and ceilings have been painted fresh white throughout to reflect the light and create a bright living space. In the main living area, these have been cladded with white bead board. The traditional wood paneling provides insulation and a decorative touch to the walls, giving an instant classic coastal feel. Light colored wood floors and an A-frame ceiling enhance the clean, airy lines of the room, which is perfect for playing games, casual family gatherings, and pottering about on rainy days and cooler evenings when outdoor life has been abandoned. Double glass doors lead off the main living room to the terrace and into the second bedroom, allowing the light to flood through the space.

The home furnishings have been kept delightfully simple with a sense of purpose and cohesion. Scandinavian antiques and local vintage finds sit alongside items inherited with the home, high-street purchases, and Danish designer pieces for a fascinating blend of old and new. The items are pared back, often with straight lines and a faint decorative touch to add interest, true to Danish heritage. Else and Keld have a keen eye for detail, which can be seen in the vignettes around the home.

Previous page, left: Simple, modern floor-to-ceiling shelving offers a carefree way to display mismatched crockery and glassware. The open style is convenient, making it easier to find things, and also creates the feeling of space.
Previous page, right: Comfortable and relaxed rattan chairs and a round table on the terrace provide an outdoor haven for family lunches alfresco.
Above left: The kitchen countertop and an open shelf serve as a handy place for storage jars, cooking utensils, and a pretty striped pitcher.
Left: Matching blue-and-white ceramics from Normann Copenhagen provide a useful place to store cooking ingredients. A simple wooden chopping board can be used as a place to cut fresh herbs or as a serving tray.
Opposite: Blue tiles with pristine white grouting perfectly match the original 1960s blue kitchen cabinetry, setting the color theme for the whole house.

The previous owners left many pieces of furniture behind, including the bench and dining chairs in the kitchen. Pretty blue-and-white striped slipcovers have been used to protect the chair seats while tying in the dining area with the rest of the home.

Life at the cottage revolves around nature and Else and Keld's home reflects this by bringing in finds from the surrounding area. A collection of sea-smoothed pebbles picked up on the nearby beach rests on top of the stove and a row of shells found on the sand runs along the windowsill. A cozy sheepskin rug and the natural, textured grain found in the light and dark wood of the bamboo and rattan furnishings add to the outdoor feel. The many windows and French doors provide natural views of the lush green garden and the trees swaying in the wind, drawing the nature inside. During the day, the doors to the terrace are thrown open, welcoming in a cool breeze.

The cottage kitchen has been recently refurbished. Despite this, the family chose to keep the statement retro blue kitchen cabinet doors that were in situ when they bought the house as they work beautifully with the crisp white walls. The delightful combination of calming white and ocean blues, a popular sequence in coastal homes, reflects the location of the home, the whites in the grains of the sand and the glistening blue of the Kattegat Sea that the family so enjoy when they are there.

The blue accent color has been picked up in various items throughout the home, such as cushions and pillows, rugs, and ceramics, bringing the interior together. A practical blue tiled splashback has been deliberately chosen to match the kitchen cabinets and add balance. Open shelving provides a useful place to store crockery, glassware, and other kitchen items. An array of chopping boards are casually propped up against the kitchen wall, adding to the easygoing feel of the home. A set of blue-and-white candy-striped dish towels has been refashioned into drapes, clipped into place using wooden clothespins for an instant, understated yet pretty window dressing that matches the coastal theme. Screening the lower part of the window in this way provides privacy while also allowing light to enter the room. The dish towels can be replaced at will, chopping and changing the pattern and color for a fresh look and feel.

Opposite: The casual open-concept kitchen in Else and Keld's cottage is the heart of the home and provides the perfect place for everyone to be together as a family.

In the dining area, a wonderful classic bench left by the previous owners dominates the space, its hard wooden seat softened with a bench cushion and throw pillows. It is a multi-functional

piece: not only does it provide seating space for more people when large gatherings are expected, but the seat lifts up to reveal storage space once used for household linen such as napkins and tablecloths. Today, the family uses it to store their favorite board games. Simple white dining chairs dressed with blue-and-white striped slipcovers sit opposite. Traditional Scandinavian rag rugs, hand woven on a loom using strips of recycled cloth in coordinating colors, are dotted about the floor to add a cozy touch.

At the far end of the room, two comfy sofas have been arranged in an L-shape around a practical square-shaped coffee table.

Above left: A handmade bamboo basket from Oi Soi Oi is used as a practical storage solution for striped outdoor cushions and adds warmth and texture to the sitting room.

Above: A game involving a wooden tray and delicate bird counters serves as a decorative piece on the coffee table.

Opposite: The sofas are made extra comfortable with a collection of blue-and-white pillows with varying patterns, including ikat, stonewash, and stripes. A large over-sized industrial-style pendant lamp from IKEA and a classic floor lamp found at a flea market light up the space in the evenings.

The family added extra windows into the gable wall to introduce more natural light to the space, making it the perfect spot to read a book, watch a film, or play a game. A large industrial-style lamp hangs over the space, punctuating the white paneled walls behind and bringing the space together.

As with many Scandinavian homes, a wood-burning stove is an essential part of everyday life in the colder months. This home is no exception. The elegant black stove is fired into action on cooler mornings, its efficiency enabling it to heat the entire cottage. The bulk of the firewood is kept in a purpose-built freestanding wood shed in the garden. The shelter keeps the wood dry, and provides plenty of storage space for a large

Above left: Intricate pitchers in varying shades of green by Danish artist Rørstand, found at a local market, have been arranged on a shelf. The white wall makes a great backdrop, allowing the unique shape of each item to be clearly seen.
Above: Pebbles from the nearby beach make a beautiful display on the wood-burning stove, their textures and colors catching the light.
Opposite: The raw nature of the cast-iron Morsøe wood-burning stove and concrete chimneybreast contrast with white walls and light wood floors to make a magnificent focal point in the main living room. Next to the fire, an antique wooden chair with cane seating provides a cozy reading corner, making the most of the natural light. A row of hooks on the wood-paneled wall behind creates a space to hang a changing array of objects, including a mirror and a basket.

sixth lamentation
William Brodrick
RAYMOND KHOURY
SANCTUARY
ENGLE DÆMONER

quantity of logs while keeping the dangers of termites and other creatures at a safe distance from the timber house. A small basket of wood for immediate use is kept indoors. The concrete chimneybreast, designed by a local, creates a dramatic backdrop. An armchair draped in a sheepskin throw, which matches the gray of the concrete, creates a charming reading corner by the fire.

On warm days, life naturally spills out into the lovely garden. The large wooden deck essentially becomes another room and provides the perfect place for breakfast, lunch, and supper alfresco on comfy, Mediterranean-style rattan chairs. Bikes lie in wait, ready for days at the beach, cycle rides along the coast, or a visit to the nearby stores.

As with many Scandinavian vacation homes, the day's activities depend on whichever way the wind is blowing, with "just being" at the top of the list. For Else and Keld, the summer cottage is the perfect place to unwind and absorb the sunlight before the summer starts to fade and the leaves turn yellow and orange.

Opposite: A limited edition lithograph by Danish artist Kristina Dam hangs on the wall in the main room. A small table is used to display an array of pretty white ceramics on a black and copper tray from House Doctor. A modern table lamp from the same store echoes the colors of the tray.
Above left: A pretty arrangement of delicate handmade Danish ceramics by Anne Black and Casalinga makes a wonderful contrast with the copper tray and demonstrates the family's love for design.

INDEX

Page numbers in **bold** refer to illustrations

PHOTOGRAPHY CREDITS

Key: a = above, b = below, c = center, l = left, r = right

All photography by James Gardiner, except as stated below:
Niki Brantmark: 158; Catherine Gratwicke: 64 l, 64 r; Peter Moore: 10 r; Steve Painter: 10 l; Mark Scott: 126 r, 127 c; Debi Treloar: 9 ac, 65 c; Kate Whitaker: 11 r; Alan Williams: 126 l; Andrew Wood: 9 bc, 94 r; Polly Wreford: 9 b, 64 c, 94 c, 95 r, 126 c, 127 r

Milkweed Barn
William Hovard
Botanical Farm for Hudson Made, www.hudsonmadeny.com

Modern Log House
Architect: Jesper Brask, www.brask-leonhardt.dk

Westwind Orchard
Fabio Chizzola and Laura Ferrara, photographer and stylist, owners of Westwind Orchard, www.westwindorchard.com
Architect: Kurt Sutherland, R.A.

Woodland Valley Cabin
The Woodland Valley Cabin was designed by Amanda Bupp and Bianca Barattini in affiliation with The Graham & Co., www.thegrahamandco.com

Lomma Country Home
Susann Larsson, purplearea.blogspot.com

Scanian Farmhouse
The interior decorations are designed by Gunilla Montan

The Hill in Vermont
Nadia Q. Dole
www.thehillworkshops.com
www.thestoreatfivecorners.com

Lakeside Retreat
Per Henriksen, owner of Franz Jaeger & Me, www.franzj.com

Hudson Farmhouse
Billinge Family, www.shipleygarden.com
Designers: Tara Mangini and Percy Bright.
www.jerseyicecreamco.com

Summer Cottage
Else and Keld Jorgensen's home in Tisvildeleje, Denmark

ACKNOWLEDGMENTS

Thank you to the team at CICO, particularly Cindy for your faith in me, and Sally, Carmel, and Kerry for your endless support and hard work. And to Gillian and Louise for your wonderful creativity and attention to detail.

To photographer extraordinaire James Gardiner for capturing the essence of Modern Pastoral, for your tremendous energy, eye for detail, and for making me laugh on the longest of days. And Andy Swannel and Holly Mallone.

This book wouldn't have been possible without the homeowners who so graciously opened their doors. Your generosity, kindness, and hospitality have been overwhelming.

To my wonderful husband Per for looking after the girls all summer so that I could write this book and for believing in me. And to my daughters Olivia and Alice and stepson Albin, who make me brim with pride and inspire me in all kinds of ways.

An enormous thank you to my parents, Barbara and Martin, who inspired my love of the countryside from an early age and have always encouraged me to follow my dreams, even if it means living miles from home. And my sisters Cassie and Charlie, my best friends.

Thank you to Bo for being my botanical encyclopedia. To Joanna Le Pluart, who has encouraged and supported me with my writing for the past decade. And to Robin, Hillary, and Gemma for looking after me on my trip to America (and for driving me to the airport at break-neck speed).

I would also like to thank my fabulous friends near and far for your positive energy and endless support.

And last but by no means least, thank you to everyone who follows my blog, without whom I would never have had this wonderful opportunity. I hope you enjoy this book as much as I have enjoyed writing it.

Niki